THE STEWARD OF SPEECH

THE STEWARD OF SPEECH

Confess, Renounce and Recall your Negative Words

Wendell Gilkey

XULON PRESS

Xulon Press
2301 Lucien Way #415
Maitland, FL 32751
407.339.4217
www.xulonpress.com

© 2022 by Wendell Gilkey

All rights reserved solely by the author. The author guarantees all contents are original and do not infringe upon the legal rights of any other person or work. No part of this book may be reproduced in any form without the permission of the author.

Due to the changing nature of the Internet, if there are any web addresses, links, or URLs included in this manuscript, these may have been altered and may no longer be accessible. The views and opinions shared in this book belong solely to the author and do not necessarily reflect those of the publisher. The publisher therefore disclaims responsibility for the views or opinions expressed within the work.

Unless otherwise indicated, Scripture quotations taken from the King James Version (KJV) – *public domain*.

Paperback ISBN-13: 978-1-6628-5734-8
Ebook ISBN-13: 978-1-6628-5735-5

Contents

Author's Note ix
Introduction xiii
Instructions xv

Chapter 1. The Way It Is 1

The Steward of Speech 1
The Power of the Spoken Word 1
Your Children 4
Eavesdropping Spirits 6
Binding Eavesdropping Spirits 6
Holy Angels 7
The Whole Armor of God, Ephesians 6:10-18 7
Ephesians 6:10-18 Comment 10
A Personal Testimony 11

Chapter 2. Testimony 15

A Prophetic Dream 17
The Dream in the Winter of 2012 18
Speaking at Churches in Africa 21
The Holy Spirit Takes Control 25
The Prayer 26

Chapter 3. Repent, Renounce, Recall, and Refrain 31

Words of Idleness 31
Words of Foolishness 32
Words without Faith 33

    Words Agreeing with the Enemy......................................34
    Words that are Blasphemous, Profane, or Untrue 37
    Words that are Unbecoming or Disparaging............................38
    All other Words that are Displeasing unto Him 39

Chapter 4. Turn It Around 45

    Confess, Repent, Renounce and Recall Unholy Words................. 46
    Keep it Clean, Stay Repented....49
    Move Forward in the Grace that has been Given You.................. 49
    Speaking in Love...52
    Intervene, Permission, Invite...53

Chapter 5. Taming the Tongue. 57

    James, Chapter 1. Verse 26..57
    James, Chapter 3. 57
    James, Chapter 4. 58
    Sins of the Tongue 59

Chapter 6. Forgiveness Commanded 63

    You are Commanded to Forgive 64
    Those that are Related or Close to You 65
    Those who are or were in Authority over You.........................65
    The Prayer of Forgiveness 66

Chapter 7. The Fear of the Lord 69

    Scriptures...69
    To Depart from Evil is Understanding 72
    Wisdom is the Primary Thing...72
    Distress and Anguish to those Who do not Fear Him 73
    A Personal Testimony 74
    The Fear of the Lord is Manifested in your Words.....................76
    The Fear of the Lord 77

Chapter 8. Word Curses 81

- Your Word Curses 81
- Curses you Inadvertently Placed upon Yourself 81
- Curses from Those that are or were in Authority 83
- Sins of the Tongue 84

Chapter 9. Prayers 89

- Take your Hands off God's Property 89
- Father, Order my Speech 90
- Faithful, Available, and Teachable 90
- Binding Eavesdropping Spirits 91
- Setting the Atmosphere 91
- Submitting your Will to the Lord 92
- The Whole Armor of God 93
- The Impenetrable Hedge of Protection 93
- Covering Our Loved Ones and Descendants 94
- Breaking off curses 94
- Breaking Free Prayer 99
- The Prayer of Forgiveness 99
- Confess the Sins of Your Tongue 100
- Binding and Loosing 101
- Defeating Words with Words 102
- Order my Steps, Govern my Life 102
- Assign your Holy Warring Angels 103

Chapter 10. The Evil Use of Tongue and Lips 109

- The Liar 110
- The Slanderer 113
- The Curser 118
- The Betrayer 124
- The Opposer 126
- The Gossip 128
- The Whisperer 130
- The Backbiter 132

The Accuser *134*
The Talebearer *136*
The Tattler *138*
The Informer *140*
The Reporter *142*
The Detractor *144*
The Disseminator *146*
The Busybody *147*
The Scoffer *149*
The Mocker *151*
The Scorner *153*
The Babbler *156*
Conclusion *161*

Final Thoughts **163**

Author's Note

Congratulations on purchasing this unique book. You are about to embark on one of the most important adventures of your life. I wish I had known about this when I was a young man, but I thank God for the revelation of this truth, now. I thank Him that I am able, through our precious Lord, to disseminate this information to you, the reader, through this book. Saints, believe me, you need to know this and put it into practice, there is healing and deliverance within the pages of this book. Memorize the prayers that are in the following pages and cleanse yourself of all the negative words that you have ever spoken. Do it for yourself first and then for your family because the words that come out of your mouth affect them just as much as they affect you.

You will learn to use your words very carefully, for you know the enemy is eavesdropping and the holy angels are recording your every word. And you WILL have to give an account for your words at your final judgment! Just look at Matthew 12:36, (but I say unto you, that every idle word men may speak they will give account of it in the day of judgment). Yes, my dear saints, you will someday stand before the judgment seat of Christ and the holy angels will bring back every idle word that you have ever spoken, and you will have to give an account for those words.

Those words are still out there, my friend

The good news is that you can renounce and recall those words and ask the angels to bring them back and bury them at the feet of Jesus. You will also at the same time be released from the negative effects of those words on yourself and your family, so you will NOT *be held accountable for those negative words at your final judgment. Those words will not even exist anymore!*

What could be more important than this?

As you do this, your speech will become clean, more so, and increasingly every day. This is an ongoing process, but you will get to the place where you just do not utter any negative words anymore.

You will be able to keep yourself clear and clean and forgiven of any negative words daily with the prayers that I have included in this book. What a place of freedom!

You will become very aware of the power of your words to affect your life either negatively or positively. You will also realize that how you speak to your children is extremely important to their well-being.

AS I GO

The information given in this book did not come out of my "vast" repository of knowledge, because I simply do not have one.

I am learning a great deal of it at the same time as I am delivering it to you.

The Holy Spirit did not "download" this book to me in a mere matter of hours. This book took over nine months to write.

AUTHOR'S NOTE

I did not have a plan or notes and prepared nothing. I only had a vague idea of what I was going to write. I did not know how long or short the book would be. I did have a title in mind and a subject, then I just showed up and started typing. I asked the Holy Spirit to give me his words, ***as I go.***

Line upon line.

Precept upon precept.

Chapter upon chapter.

Verse upon verse.

I am delivering to you what was delivered to me.

Jeremiah 29:11

For I know the plans I have for you saith the Lord. Plans to help you and not to harm you. Plans to give you a hope and a future.

Jeremiah 33:3

Call unto me and I will answer and show you great and mighty things that you know not thereof.

Introduction

Your life will change dramatically when the Lord washes away your negative words in the blood of His precious Son, Jesus Christ never to be remembered against you again.

In the following pages, I reveal to you what the Holy Spirit revealed to me, most miraculously. I had no idea about this subject, I did not know that it was possible to wash corrupt speech away. I knew that every idle word that I had ever spoken would be brought up to me to account for in my final judgment, but I had no idea of what to do about it. That always bothered me and the fact that I just kept adding to them, increasing the count of my negative words every day made it seem so futile. What could be done about it? I prayed and prayed for the Lord to correct my speech, I knew the power of my spoken words, and I was ashamed that I just could not seem to get ahold of my tongue. This is common to all men and women. You are not alone in this, my friend.

Now, I have overcome him by the blood of the Lamb and the word of my testimony, see Revelation 12:11. I have been released! It feels so good. You will get a good education from this book, and you will be released as well.

Why have I not heard this teaching before? I have been to many church services, but I never heard anything like this. It is my sincere prayer that the pastors and clergy will embrace this and pass it on to their congregations.

Once you hear this, it should resonate in your spirit as truth, and I pray that you will seriously consider this and never let go of it. Your well-being and salvation, as well as the well-being and salvation of your loved ones and descendants, is my only goal.

So read on my dear friends, you will be amazed.

Instructions

How to use this book

After having read this book through, I recommend that you start by repenting for all the negative and unholy words that you have ever spoken over your entire lifetime. This is easier than you think since most of them are the same words used repeatedly. Just ask the Holy Spirit to help you and he will. When I first did this, I just started on my own and I did it in a chronological fashion starting from my earliest youth up to the present. That was "my" way, but "His" way was better, He pressed upon me to ask the Holy Spirit to help me and to lead me in this endeavor. This was only to lead and help me and not to take over. Realize that you cannot ask Him to do it for you, and you cannot do it all on your own either, together with the Lord wins the race.

When He "granted" me this repentance, The Holy Spirit began to lead me every morning in the sequence and way that I was to address these unholy words. I did not proceed chronologically but in the way the Holy Spirit led me. I found that although it was for a lifetime of unholy words, they were mostly the same words used repeatedly so the task was not as overwhelming as I first thought. I asked for His help, gave Him permission to intervene, and invited Him in. (please do not ever forget the three power words; intervene, permission, and invite.) **He led me from place to place convicting me of my word transgressions.** I was also enlightened, as I went, as to the exact nature of my word transgressions and why my words were not suitable to Him. I learned about the way my parents talked to me and how I just automatically talked to my children the same way. I also learned about word curses that I had been placing on myself and others in ignorance, as well as the word curses that others had, without malice, in most cases, placed upon me.

I was brought to the realization that it is a sin to disparage others who are indeed made in his image. It is a sacred privilege that we have been given to even be able to use words, just as the creator does. I learned how not to agree with the enemy. To speak in faith, not to use language that is unbecoming of the man or woman of God that you are. Never disparage yourself. How to quit using blasphemous, profane, or untrue words. How to literally bite my tongue when tempted to utter unholy words. How to be slow to speak and to weigh my words carefully. How to refrain from words that are idle or foolish. How to refrain from all other words that are displeasing unto Him. How to stop yourself from uttering the unholy words of judgment. How to stop disparaging talk about other groups and peoples.

The key to perfection in language is found in the fear of the Lord. Chapter 7 will instruct you in this discipline. Without it, your language will be flawed. The only way to achieve total victory over your tongue is found in the fear of the Lord.

1. Read this entire book.
2. Start repenting for your unholy words.
3. Use the prayers that are in chapter 9.
4. Now that you are clean, stay repented daily.
5. Turn it around, speak in love.
6. Stay in the Word of God.

God bless you.

2nd Chronicles 7:14

If my people that are called by my name will humble themselves and pray and seek my face, and turn from their wicked ways, then I will hear from Heaven, answer their prayers, and heal their land.

What to expect

You will undoubtedly see your speech being cleansed and cleared of all words that are displeasing unto the Lord. You will notice progress right away but remember this is a process, it is not a one and your done kind of thing. I wish it were as easy as praying "Lord, I ask you to clean my words so that they may be pleasing unto you from now on, Amen." That, my friend, just will not "cut" it. This, as I have laid it out, will however cut it. It did it for me, and those that I have shared it with, and it will do it for you.

As you go through this, you can expect to receive revelation knowledge about your words both positive and negative. You will also gain a deep insight into not only your speech but also the words of others whom you interact with. You will see the simplicity of dismissing negative words, this is not a complicated teaching.

Imagine how you will feel when you have mastered your tongue. It is a place of freedom that the enemy of your soul cannot penetrate. Now, you can instruct many. It is the true joy of the release of bondage.

> **Do you even realize it?**
> ***The enemy has kept you in bondage,***
> ***speaking words that pleased him!***

It is extremely important to the enemy to corrupt your speech because if he can get you to use unholy, profane, blasphemous words, that will be your "testimony" about your very own self, out of your own mouth. You are damning yourself in real-time and you are damning your children and the others that you have spoken ill of. Your testimony can be an extremely positive confession, or it can be an extremely negative confession. It can influence you and your family for good or for evil. Know this!

Can you see the enormity of your confession? I pray beloved saints, that the power of darkness will be broken over your tongue. In the chapter titled "Turn it around," you can expect to learn how to speak in love. How to repent for negative words daily to keep yourself forgiven; you will no longer have to give an account for those negative words at your final judgment. These words will simply not even exist anymore.

Goals

1. To comprehend and understand the power of your words, and that they *will bear fruit*, either positively or negatively.
2. To know that the Lord has shown his Holy Glory Light to illuminate your words and the way that you have conducted yourself in speech. *This is not to condemn you*; this is to enlighten you as to the nature of the words that you have spoken so that you can know what you must do to overcome your ungodly words.
3. To realize the fact that others have spoken to you negatively, probably not in malice, but in ignorance, these "word curses" have negatively affected you and must be broken off.
4. To know that your negative words have affected others just as their negative words, to you, affected you.
5. Realize the fact that the words from your very own mouth about yourself are the most damning testimony against you. This must end immediately.
6. Understand forgiveness and go through your life forgiving all who have trespassed against you regarding the words that they have uttered. Whether they be truth, lies, slander, or a mixture thereof.
7. To gain new insight into the enormous power that you have in your mouth. Learning to speak in love and truth.

8. To enjoy your new freedom and victory. To help others to understand this teaching. To spread the word and move forward.
9. To enter into a close personal relationship with the Lord, in prayer. Trust in the Lord, he is your best friend.

The author with his son and daughter

Proverbs 18:21
Death and life are in the power of the tongue: and they that love it will eat the fruit thereof.

Chapter 1.
THE WAY IT IS

The Steward of Speech

I know you steward everything the Lord has given you. Your family, home, automobile, health, finances, workplace, business, and everything that you have been blessed with.

Have you ever considered your speech? You have been given this divine gift from your creator. You are made in his image and have the power to use words, all of which bear fruit, either positively or negatively. This book will enlighten you about this truth. By the time you finish it, you will truly be a "steward of your speech." You will instruct your children as well as others and move forward in a quantum leap.

The Power of Your Spoken Word

You are made in the image of God. He framed the entire universe with his words. He gave you the power to use your words to both bless and curse. You must be careful not to curse because your words contain immense power. The power to create, change circumstances, encourage, and heal as well as the power to destroy and cause damage, hurt, pain and suffering.

You can curse your very own life with your words and many people do, not knowing that self-induced curses are born in this manner.

Proverbs 22:6
Train up a child in the way he should go and when he is old, he will not depart from it.

Proverbs 3:12
For whom the Lord loveth he correcteth; even as a father the son in whom he delighteth.

Colossians 3:21
Fathers provoke not your children to anger lest they be discouraged.

Ephesians 6:4
And ye fathers, provoke not your children to wrath: But bring them up in the nurture and admonition of the Lord.

Your Children

You can also curse your children with your words without even realizing it. *It is you who are in authority over their very lives*. That is an awesome responsibility, one that you will undoubtedly have to account for at your final judgment.

This being "the way it is" you must never, under any circumstances speak derogatory or disparaging words to your children. To do so is to curse them. they will, unfortunately, begin to resemble those remarks, or they will, fortunately, begin to respond to the positive remarks. Remember it is all in the power of:

Your very own tongue!
*Proverbs 18:21 Death and life are in the power of the tongue:
and they that love it will eat the fruit thereof.*

Notice that Proverbs 18:21 states "the power of the tongue." So, no matter how angry you become with your children, do not ever say things like "your stupid" or "look what you've done, you brat." Or "how dumb can you be?" "I wish I never had you." There is a whole list of these kinds of words. What you may not have known is the far-reaching negative effects that it has on them and that you are… ***calling out to misfortune…*** when you speak like that. There is a real danger in speaking to your children in this manner, it must stop immediately! Where have you heard that before? You probably have not. I know that I had not, in my life, heard this until I spoke it out in a church service in Africa. The words that I spoke to them that night bypassed my brain, and I only had a vague idea of what I was saying. The Holy Spirit took control of my words, as I stood in the pulpit in Africa. I learned this at the same time as the congregation did.

Proverbs 10:22

Whom the Lord makes rich is rich indeed and he adds no sorrow with it.

Eavesdropping Spirits

Are you aware that your enemy, the Devil, has eavesdropping spirits that are listening to every word you say? That is just "the way it is."

Remember the old saying "knock on wood"? People still use that saying today "Just in case the Devil is listening." For example, "I have not had a cold in over two years, knock on wood."

I have news for you, the Devil *is* listening but knocking on wood is not going to save you. You must bind the eavesdropping spirits of the enemy, Those, that are assigned to you and yours today. I do this every day.

> **Since I have been praying this, I know that I
> have the freedom to speak as I will!**

I have left you a prayer, the one that I use every single day to keep the enemy at bay in this regard. You will find it here as well as in the prayer section of this book.

Binding Eavesdropping Spirits

Lord Jesus, I thank you for taking me off the enemy's radar and off his frequency. I ask you to scramble my words today to you in prayer, as well as my words to myself or to anyone else, both oral and written, so that the enemy cannot eavesdrop on me and understand any of my communication.

I now bind the enemy's eavesdropping spirits, those assigned to me and mine today. I bind you spirits now, in the name of Jesus Christ and cast you into the pit. I seal you in there with the blood of Christ.

I now loose the opposite spirits from Heaven into our lives instead. I lose the seven-fold spirit of the Lord and the Holy Spirit. Thank you, Jesus. Amen.

Holy Angels

The holy angels are recording every single word that you say. Those words of yours, every one of them, are still floating through the universe, your corrupt words are out there and quite available to the holy angels to gather up in nets and bring back to Jesus. You will have to give an account for those words at your final judgment. That is "just the way it is."

> *Matthew 12:36 But I say to you, that every idle word men may speak they will give an account of in the day of judgment.*

The good news is that you can repent for, renounce, and recall those words and ask the Lord to wash them away in the blood of His precious Son, Jesus Christ, never to be remembered against you again. Once again, I did not know this, and I had never heard anything like it before. I did however speak this out at another church service that I was preaching in Africa. Those words also bypassed my brain, and I only had a vague recollection of what I was teaching the congregants. I have left you a prayer, in chapter 9, of this book under the sub-title (Confess the sins of your tongue.) This is the one that I use every day to keep myself clear, clean, and forgiven for any corrupt communication that might come out of my mouth. Just in case.

The Whole Armor of God, Ephesians 6:10-18

Finally, my brethren, be strong in the Lord, and in the power of his might.

Put on the whole armor of God, that ye may be able to stand against the wiles of the Devil.

For we wrestle not against flesh and blood but against principalities, against powers, against the rulers of the darkness of this world, against spiritual wickedness in high places.

Wherefore take unto you the whole armor of God, that ye may be able to withstand in the evil day, and having done all, to stand...

Stand therefore, having your loins girt about with truth, and having on the breastplate of righteousness.

And your feet shod with the preparation of the gospel of peace.

Above all, taking the shield of faith, wherewith ye shall be able to quench all the fiery darts of the wicked.

And take the helmet of salvation, and the sword of the Spirit, which is the Word of God:

Praying always with all prayer and supplication in the spirit and watching thereunto with all perseverance and supplication for all saints.

Proverbs 4:20-22

My son attend to my words, incline thine ear to my sayings, do not let them depart from your eyes. Keep them in the midst of thine heart for they are life to those who find them and health to all their flesh.

Ephesians 6:10-18 Comment

The above is the apostle Paul's letter to the church in Ephesus, notice he is letting them know that they do have an adversary and his name is the Devil. He is telling them to put on the whole armor of God so that they may be able to stand against all the "wiles" of the Devil. Brothers and sisters, I wish that you did not have an adversary and enemy, but you do.

You cannot behave as if he does not exist because he certainly does. Your Bible very clearly states it here.

The second paragraph states that we wrestle not against flesh and blood, but against principalities, against powers, and against the rulers of the darkness of this world. Against spiritual wickedness in high places. I have found this to be true.

I have conflicted with people that I could see were very plainly being animated by the powers in the second heaven.

I have even been warned by the Lord, "that is not my son" or "that is not my daughter," while in the heat of conflict and that we wrestle not against flesh and blood. Lest I get angry and say things that I should not. So, take the whole armor of God so that you may be able to withstand in the evil day, and having done all to stand, stand.

The third paragraph lists the armor that you put on. "With your loins girt about with truth." This is a belt of truth.

Having on the breastplate of righteousness and your feet shod with the preparation of the Gospel of Peace. You must familiarize yourself with the Bible's teachings because that is how you defeat your enemy.

Remember when Satan had Jesus up on the mountain just after his baptism? How did he defeat Satan? By quoting the scriptures in response to all of Satan's questions and comments.

A Personal Testimony

Some years ago, I was in the hospital in a town not far from where I lived. I had pneumonia and I had already been there for about five days. I was feeling better now, and I wanted to go home. I was waiting for the doctor to come into my room, I was sure that he would release me.

He finally came in and I told him that I was ok now and ready to leave. He did not agree and told me that I would have to stay just one more day. I was so upset and disappointed. Just after he walked out, my cellphone rang, and it was the landlord from the apartments where I lived.

She did not know that I was in the hospital, she thought I was in my apartment. She asked me if I had been using the washers and dryers on the other side of the parking lot. I told her; "No, I haven't used them, I realize that those belong to the people in those other apartments, I know better than that." I was already in a bad mood trying to process what the doctor told me. I probably should not have even picked up the phone.

Then she just tore into me and said that the people on that side of the parking lot saw your cleaning lady using them and that she had your laundry and went into your apartment with it.

I replied that I did not even have a cleaning lady. Now my blood was boiling. I told her that I had not even been there for about a week. Then I took a deep breath, and I was going to spew on her everything that I could. I was going to yell at her at the top of my lungs, maybe even cuss her out or at least call her a bunch of names. Just then I heard in my spirit "that is not my daughter." I heard it so loud that it shocked me, and as soon as I heard that I immediately realized that this poor woman was being manipulated by the powers in the second heaven, the powers, and the principalities that Paul talked about in Ephesians 6:10. The enemy caught me at the exact right moment that I was vulnerable because I was so upset about having to stay another day in the hospital, and then she started "barking" at me about using someone else's washer and dryer!

I was arrested right there on the spot, I slowly let my breath out… and very calmly said. "Well, I have not even been there for about a week but it sure is nice to know that someone is looking out for me in my absence, thank you so much." To which she said, "You're welcome, Wendell."

If I would have yelled and screamed at her I would have regretted it, after getting to know her better, I found out that she was a saint of the most-high God and that she had extensive knowledge of the word of God.

Sometime later, I asked her, "Why are you so tough and negative with everybody here?" She told me; "My true nature is to be very kind and helpful, but if these people knew that about me, they would run me over like a freight train. It is a self-preservation technique that I use, so whenever someone asks me for something, I automatically say, **NO!**"

The seven-fold spirit of the Lord:

The spirit of the Lord.
The spirit of wisdom and understanding.
The spirit of counsel and might.
The spirit of knowledge.
The fear of the Lord.

Matthew 5:14-16

Ye are the light of the world, A city that is set on a hill cannot be hid.

Neither do men light a candle, and put it under a bushel, but on a candlestick; and it giveth light unto all that are in the house.

Let your light so shine before men, that they may see your good works, and glorify your Father which is in heaven.

Chapter 2.

Testimony

I received this revelation from the Lord, of the immense power of words to shape our lives and the lives of our descendants. The Lord revealed to me the many truths that I have brought forward here in this book. When you read it, it will resonate in your spirit as divine truth. My sincere prayer is that you are able to receive it.

The incredible story of how this teaching was divinely revealed to me is in the following pages. In 2012 I had several prophetic dreams indicating that our words are seemingly immortal. They do not just drop to the ground; they are floating through the universe. So, I knew those words, both positive and negative, are all still out there. I had no idea of what to do about all the negative words that bore witness against me at that time.

Then some two years later in 2014, I had an opportunity to go to Africa and preach in some churches there. The Holy Spirit revealed to me through the words of my very own mouth, that we can indeed **confess, repent, renounce, and recall** those words so that they can never be used against us anymore and so that we would not have to give an account for them at our final judgment.

Daniel 11:32,33

And such as do wickedly against the covenant shall he corrupt by flatteries: **but the people that do know their God shall be strong and do exploits.**

And they that understand among the people shall instruct many: yet they shall fall by the sword, and by flame, by captivity, and by spoil, many days.

A Prophetic Dream

Some years ago, I had a prophetic dream about words that were spoken, and how they were strung together on clay tablets about five inches square. They appeared in sentences that came out of the people's mouths and just floated in front of them for about a minute before going out from them. The strings of clay tablets seemed to float as if in water. Swaying back and forth, up, and down.

As the words began to float away, I saw them leave the building either through the walls or the ceiling. I remember wondering, "Where are these words going?"

This entire prophetic dream is documented for you in the pages below titled: "The dream in the winter of 2012."

It was sometime later that the Lord impressed upon me that those strings of words are going out into the universe, and they will be recoverable by the holy angels at the person's final judgment, either to be used against them or in their favor, as they kneel at the feet of Jesus. I still did not know that we have the ability to renounce and recall the ungodly, unholy words that we have spoken.

At that time, I just thought whatever has been said, is already said, we can ask forgiveness for those words and try to order our speech so that we do not add to them, but nothing more.

I found out while preaching a church service in Africa, that we do indeed have the God-given power to renounce and recall those negative words. I found this out at the same time as the congregation. The Holy Spirit spoke this out through me, and I only had a vague idea of what I was saying!

The Dream in the Winter of 2012

I had a prophetic dream about the healing rooms in my area. This is a place where the saints of God pray for the sick that they will recover. I dreamed that I was present in the healing rooms that night. I witnessed the practitioners in a praise, worship, and communion service just before the arrival of the sick. I remember trying to talk to some of them and they just ignored me. I began to realize that they could not see or hear me and that I was there in the spirit only and not in body, just as an observer. At that time, I had no concept of being able to observe in the spirit.

There were about seven healing practitioners that night. When they finished communion, I observed one of the sisters get up and stand behind each one of them, as they were seated, she anointed each one, on the forehead with olive oil with her thumb. She then laid hands on each one of them in turn, praying for power and anointing, calling down the Kingdom of God and the will of God.

As she went from one person to another, I noticed discomfort on each of their faces. It looked as though they were all sick to their stomachs. When she finished, they all began to heave and all at the same time they spewed forth something from their mouths. I hurried across the room to see what it was. To my surprise, they all spewed out words that just hung in the air in front of them, in strings of sentences written on what appeared to be clay tablets. I remember thinking that I could just reach out and pick up one of those sentences, they were as real as the people that uttered them. I then watched as the sentences floated away. I knew those words were out there, in the universe. This was in 2012, two years before I went to Africa. This was the first part of the revelation.

The second part of the revelation did not occur until the passing of two years, it occurred in 2014, as I was preaching at a church in Africa, I spoke it out without knowing what I was saying. I already knew those words both positive and negative were definitely out there in the universe, and recoverable by the holy angels. Now I knew that you can **renounce and recall** the negative words. I also realized that is just *how* we *will be held accountable* for every idle word. This story is presented to you in the following pages.

Proverbs 3:13,14

Happy is the man that findeth wisdom, and that getteth understanding for the merchandise of it is better than the merchandise of silver and the gain thereof than fine gold.

Isaiah 3:10

Say to the righteous, that it shall be well with him: for they shall eat the fruit of their doings.

Speaking in Churches in Africa

Two years after the prophetic dream, in the spring of 2014, I had the opportunity to go to Africa. I went to Africa by myself. I knew a pastor there, when he would come to Texas, He would always stay at my residence.

On my second night there I was scheduled to preach at a rather large church. The only thing is I am not a preacher. I had never preached before anywhere. When the pastor told me this I was stunned. I told him I do not have anything to preach about. He insisted and gave me time to prepare a sermon, which I did. I came up with a bunch of notes on forgiveness and repentance. I practiced it in my room. I do not have a problem with getting up and talking in a crowded room but to produce a one-hour sermon, that might be a problem, it was.

That night he introduced me, and I got up and greeted them and began my "preaching career." I lasted about 15 minutes and I did not have anything else to say on those subjects. So, I told them "That is all I have, thank you very much for this opportunity." Then I just sat down. The pastor freaked out. He said, "get back up there! You must go for at least forty-five more minutes." I refused. I told him the truth "that *is* all I have." He got up very quickly and "saved the day." He very skillfully went on with the sermon for the night.

I was devastated, and embarrassed. He was extremely disappointed in me. *Strike one!* On the way back to my hotel he told me that he had been telling these people for several months that there is a great man of God from Texas that is going to be coming here because he is burning with a word for you people. A great prophet is coming here. Although I can walk in the office of a prophet, I have never spoken one word that the Lord did not tell me. I was expected to deliver a "word" to these people individually also. Well, unless led by God to do so, I will not.

He told me he was going to leave me in the hotel the entire day tomorrow by myself so that I could come up with a sermon for that night. He left me his laptop and said, "If you can't come up with a sermon, get one off the internet." He showed me what websites to look at. He said "Pick a subject such as the woman with the issue of blood, or David and Goliath or just any of the stories in the Bible and expound on it enough to make it last at least one hour."

That very night I was taken to another church, where I did exactly the same thing as the night before. I did manage to last about 25 minutes. But I had to say that is all I have and sit back down, he had to jump up there and finish it. I found out that he also was depending on the donations that would be given him from the churches for each of my "appearances." I was damaging his reputation as well as his finances. This was not what I expected to be doing in Africa. I had no idea that this is what he had in mind for me. *Strike two.*

Well, the third night out was just a repeat of the first two nights. He had me scheduled to deliver a sermon almost every night. By now I was done and so was he. This just did not work out for either one of us. *Strike three!* I was out!

He got me the next night and took me to a church for round four. (Which surprised me.) I had not "prepared a sermon" and I did not even care to. I planned to just get up and bless the people and sit back down. As we were driving down the street in the car, He asked me "Well, what are you going to preach on tonight?" I replied, "I have no idea." He freaked out and started yelling at me. I simply told him, "Well, pastor, I will get up and say what I can and if I fail again, I will just sit back down and let you finish it." By now I just wanted to go back to Texas so badly. I wanted out of there!

When we arrived, he introduced me, I stepped up onto the platform and blessed the people, and then a strange thing happened. I started talking without even thinking!

Then the Lord put forth his hand and touched my mouth and the Lord said unto me Behold I have put my words in your mouth. Jeremiah 1:9

I would say something, the interpreter would interpret it and then look back at me for the next line. I would come up with the next line but the words I spoke bypassed my brain. I kept going. This was entirely unexpected. I had no idea of what to say next but by the time the interpreter

Looked back at me it just came out. There was one time that she looked back at me for the next line, and I sort of panicked I did not even know what subject we were on let alone what to say next. I had a picture in my head of Peter walking on the water and then getting scared and sinking. I trusted the Holy Spirit to keep me going. I kept my eyes on Jesus. I spoke for well over an hour. There was a "holy hush" over the church and the people were writing down everything they could on their notepads. This was the first service where I told the people that they had the power to renounce and recall their negative words. This was the first service that I chastised them for speaking negatively to their children. Here I had been at the end of my rope having failed to deliver a sermon three times already. I had no intention of delivering a sermon that night. I was just going to bless the congregation and sit back down. The Lord had other plans for me though. He waited for me to surrender. Then by his might and not mine, I heard directly from the Holy Spirit.

They knew that the Holy Spirit was indeed talking to them and not me.

The author and his interpreter at an evening church service in Kampala, Uganda.
This was the first time that the Holy Spirit spoke through him.

The Holy Spirit Takes Control

The next church I went to was on a Sunday morning, a rather large church. They introduced me and I stepped onto the platform and the same thing happened. I let the Holy Spirit use me to speak to these people. We already saw what my capabilities were, practically nothing. I prepared absolutely nothing for this Sunday sermon. I let the Holy Spirit take complete control of me. I preached for about an hour and 15 minutes. I told them all kinds of things and even many things that I did not even know myself until I spoke them. When I finished, I was talking with the pastor of that church when he asked me. "Did you prepare this sermon before you came here this morning?" I told him "Absolutely not, I had no idea of what I was going to tell you people." He told me that about 12 years ago a man came through there that did the same thing, just let the Holy Spirit take full control.

He said, "You are the first one in over 12 years that I have seen do that, but I recognized it." He asked me if the pastor that brought me there told me about any of the problems they were having at the church. I replied, "No, I was unaware of any problems here." He told me "You were right in addressing my assistants in what you told them." (I instructed and even scolded some of his assistants.)

I preached in other churches while I was there, and I prepared nothing. I just let the Holy Spirit tell them what *he* wanted to tell them not what I wanted to tell them. All these churches wanted me back, but I was scheduled elsewhere.

This is taken from my book "A Call to Prayer." If you do not have a copy of this book, I highly recommend that you obtain one. The things that I spoke about in those churches in Africa are all in that book. I documented them and put them away, but I had no idea that I would someday author a book on this subject. The reason that I have authored *this* book all have to do with the fact that the saints need to wake up to these truths. I have been given a great light and it needs to be set upon a lampstand for all to see.

The Prayer

Lord God, I confess the sins of my tongue over the past day/days. I confess all words that I spoke that were:

Words of idleness.

Words of foolishness.

Words without faith.

Words that were agreeing with the enemy.

All words that were blasphemous, profane, or untrue.

I confess all words that were unbecoming of me.

I confess all words that were disparaging to myself.

I confess any and all other words that were displeasing unto you.

I confess them as sin, and I repent of them. I now *renounce* each and every word that was not right, in your eyes, Lord.

I *recall* these words from floating through the universe and I send a detail of holy angels out to gather them up in nets and bring them back and bury them at the feet of Jesus.

I ask to be forgiven for these unfortunate words as I forgive myself for uttering them. I ask that they all be washed away by the blood of your precious Son, Jesus Christ never to be remembered against me again. And so that I will not be held accountable for these words at my final judgment, because *they do not even exist anymore,* even now.

Amen.

The author and his interpreter at a Sunday morning church service in Kampala, Uganda. No notes. No preparation, he just let the Holy Spirit tell them, through him, what the Spirit had to share with the congregation.

Matthew 12:36,37

But I say unto you, that every idle word that men shall speak, they shall give account thereof in the day of judgment.

For by thy words thou shalt be justified, and by thy words, thou shalt be condemned.

Chapter 3.

Repent, Renounce, Recall, and Refrain

The four "R's"

Words of Idleness

Any words that you did not mean are words of idleness, for example, you could say "I hate my mother," in a moment of anger but of course, you do not hate her *but yet you said it!* This is a dangerous statement, and it must be repented for, and those idle words must be renounced and recalled, if you do not do this, those words will float through the universe and eventually be gathered up by the holy angels and brought to your final judgment. You will indeed have to give an account for those words to the righteous King of the universe as you kneel before Him, on the day of your final judgment.

Another example of idle speech would be "I wish I was dead!" Have you ever said that? You know your enemy the Devil is eavesdropping on you through his eavesdropping spirits, and they may try to make that a reality. You and the Lord as well as the Devil know that you really did not mean it, yet you used your divine gift of speech to curse your very own self.

The enemy could very well say; "That is his testimony out of his very own mouth about himself." This is a profoundly serious transgression, and you need to confess, repent, renounce, and recall those dangerous words, and refrain from using that kind of language.

Words of Foolishness

Many people joke around in humor, but at times, it can get awfully close to "foolish talk." It is called foolish talk for good reason because a fool does talk like that. Believe me, you do not want to be that person, what does the Bible say about that?

> *A fool is unwise, lacks sense, and lacks judgment. Fools do not want to know the truth. They laugh at the truth and turn their eyes away from the truth.*

Proverbs 18:2 A fool hath no delight in understanding, but that his heart may discover itself.

Proverbs 1:7 The fear of the Lord is the beginning of knowledge: but fools despise wisdom and instruction.

Proverbs 18:7 A fool's mouth is his destruction, and his lips are the snare of his soul.

Some examples of foolish talk can include absurd statements such as "I'm going to pick that car up and throw it." Or absurd boasting such as "I can do 500 push-ups in one set." Maybe you have heard statements indicating a complete lack of judgment, such as "I'm going in there and throwing all of them out." Remember a fool's mouth is his destruction.

They are always "shooting off their mouths." They often pay for it by being pillaged, plundered, beatings, and problems with the authorities. It is all a matter of using their tongue incorrectly.

They do not realize that words are indeed sacred.

They also do not have the fear of the Lord. They have misused their gift from God. Refrain from "words of foolishness."

Words without Faith

I have seen people sabotage their very own prayers with faithless words. Maybe they have been praying for a new job but then in frustration say something like "Oh, I know I will never get a new job, I will be stuck at this one forever." Well, that is all they had to say. Sometimes the Lord is testing your faith. If he is, you have just failed the test. When you fail a test, you will have to take it over again. Oftentimes your breakthrough is just around the corner, and you have, after all your "standing" just jeopardized it with your faithless words. I have done this and lost my opportunity, but I have also been guilty of this and in his mercy, I have been granted forgiveness and did receive my reward. Imagine how bad I felt when the Lord did not punish me as I deserved. Words without faith are a detriment to your well-being as well as the well-being of your descendants and loved ones. Be slow to speak and be careful of your speech. Do not speak out in anger or frustration because so much depends on your words.

Words that are Agreeing with the Enemy.

Your enemy, the Devil, is very cunning. He will set up different circumstances for you to agree with him. Many times, when speaking to others, the spiritual wickedness in high places will animate those others to say things that cause you to agree with them. I remember, one time I was at the doctor's office and the doctor told me: "You know, this disease is going to kill you." (I thought what a horrible thing for a doctor to say to his patient.) Yet, I did reply "Yes, I know, doctor, but I'm doing the best I can." I immediately knew that I had been "had." I regretted that statement instantly. Yet I spoke those words out of my own mouth. That was my "testimony" regarding myself. I had been tricked into saying that, yet, I did say it. By the time I got out to the parking lot the Holy Spirit convicted me, I felt so bad about saying that when I did not even mean it. I just blurted it out without thinking. Ensnared by my own words. I just agreed with the enemy!

Not that the doctor was an enemy, He probably thought he was right, or he would not have said it. I should have kept my mouth shut, but the doctor was saying so many negative things before that statement that I was a little "rattled" by the time he said what he did, and it sparked the unfortunate words that I just blurted out. I have noticed a pattern like this, where the enemy gets you all worked up and then you end up "blurting" something out without thinking. So be aware of this "trick." Your adversary the Devil is the trickster of the ages.

I immediately went into prayer right in the parking lot in my car. I repented for my negative words and asked that they be washed away in the blood of His precious Son, Jesus Christ never to be remembered against me again. So that I would not have to give an account of those words at my final judgment because now I knew that they did not even exist anymore.

Thank you, Jesus. Come to find out about two years later that I did not even have that disease!

About three months later, I was in the hospital and when they released me, I had to have oxygen. I was on oxygen for about three months and I asked another doctor "When am I going to be able to get off this oxygen?" He told me these very words: "You will be on it for the rest of your life, just count on it." My mind went back to the episode of the previous doctor telling me that this disease is going to kill me, and I was prompted by the Holy Spirit not to say "ok" or agree to that in any way. I just kept my mouth shut but in my "inner man" I said, "I do not receive that." As it turned out, just a few weeks later I was able to give up the oxygen for good. That was years ago and today I have normal blood oxygen readings, thank you, Jesus.

Psalm 118:17
I shall live and not die and declare the works of the Lord.

Psalm 118:7
The Lord taketh my part with them that help me, therefore shall I see my desire upon my enemy.

Since we are "relational beings" when we talk to family and friends, we will often time recount what is going on in our lives. I have found this also to be a hidden snare in that you will undoubtedly be confronted with numerous questions like for instance "What did the doctor say?" Or "what did your boss say?" Be careful, wise, and slow to reply because sometimes those questions can be cleverly disguised *bait* for you to take. Not that these people are working for the enemy, it is just human nature, and I am sure they mean no malice with it. "Be wise as serpents and harmless as doves."

I have given much information to people, people that I should not have. Some of these people are just combing through this information to find something to "hang" you with. Or even to use to slander you at some point. Be careful who you share anything with. Best to be slow to speak and reserved. Choose your words carefully and your friends even more so. Let your words be few.

Words that are Blasphemous, Profane, or Untrue.

Unfortunately, we all have uttered words of this nature, even though we are born-again Christians. We are engaged in an ongoing struggle to tame our tongues. It is a fight, indeed a war, it is not as easy as saying "I bind all words that are not of God from ever coming off my tongue." I wish it were that easy, but it is not. That prayer just will not "cut it." What I am showing you here in this book will cut it. It did it for me, and it will do it for you. This taming of your tongue is an ongoing process.

What happens when the enemy probes you? By probing, I mean what if he stuck a sharp pencil in your ribs? Would you cuss and swear? What is going to come out of your mouth then? We all know he is not going to stick a pencil in your ribs, but he does have other ways to find out what is in your heart. What is in your heart will always come out of your mouth *when you are probed.* See Matthew 12:34.

If you drop a glass jar full of spaghetti sauce on the floor and it breaks into a million pieces, are you just going to say, "Oh no!" Or are you going to go into a tirade of profanity? I remember my mother would not utter one word of blasphemy or profanity in a case like that. She mastered her tongue at an early age. I have seen good Christian people that when faced with such a disastrous mess would blurt out profane words. Hold your tongue, bite it if you must. Start putting more of the word of God in your heart so that when probed it automatically comes out of your mouth instead.

Our words can justify us or condemn us. Make it a goal of yours to be able to withstand a probing.

> **The last thing the Devil wants to hear when he probes you is the word of God.**

Resist the Devil and he will flee from you. Remember Matthew 12:34, the words of Jesus. "Out of the abundance of the heart, the mouth speaks," when evil resides in the heart, it will be exposed in perverse speech, language contrary to the truth of God and to love.

Words that are Unbecoming or Disparaging

Any words that are unbecoming or even disparaging to you must be avoided. After all, you are a child of God. He sees you in a much better light than you see yourself. If you are a man or woman of God, act like it. Never engage in course jokes or foul language. Never say anything disparaging about yourself. Some people cope by saying disparaging things about themselves, such as "I can't do that." "I'm just an average, simple person." "I could not figure any of that out." "I'm not that smart." These are demeaning words spoken by you, a king of the King. How could you ever say those things about yourself if you truly believe that you are a king of the King? If that is you, STOP IT NOW!

I know pastors that are only regular guys until Sunday morning church and then they put on airs of a "reverend" and act like a man of God, only to go home and watch the game and drink some beer like everybody else. Their speech, corrupted. If you are a man or woman of God, you must never under any circumstances have to "put on airs." You must conduct yourself whether at church or at home in a manner befitting the man or woman of God that you truly are. He is the righteous King of the universe, and you are representing Him here on Earth. If you truly do represent Him, then act like it 100% of the time.

All Other Words that are Displeasing unto Him.

We covered everything except any and all *other* words that are displeasing unto God. These include words that you have spoken that disparage others or judge others such as saying negative things about certain peoples or groups. (Even though you may not agree with them.) You know full well that all men were created in his image. If that is so then you just spoke negatively about somebody that is made in the image of God, **thereby insulting their maker.** That is not going to go well for you, and it needs to stop. You can disagree vehemently with them and be very passionate in your opposition to them without disparaging them or calling them names. Your words can be a snare unto you or a blessing. *Do not be baited* into uttering words that are unbecoming of not only you but your fellow man. Learn to speak in love. Refrain from all forms of gossiping, talebearing, and talking about people behind their backs.

Refrain from lies and slander about others. Do not "drop" innuendos or insinuations about people to others, to color their opinions in a negative manner. Unless you need to issue a "warning," speak about others as if they were in the room with you.

All blessings to you saints of God.

Luke 10:19

Behold I give unto you power to tread on scorpions and serpents, and over all the power of the enemy, and nothing shall by any means hurt you.

1ˢᵗ John 4:4

You are of God, little children, and have overcame them for greater is he that is in you, than he that is in the world.

1ˢᵗ John 3:8,9

He that committeth sin is of the Devil: for the Devil sinneth from the beginning. **For this purpose, the Son of God was manifested, that he might destroy the works of the devil.**

Whosoever is born of God doth not commit sin; for his seed remaineth in him: and he cannot sin, because he is born of God.

The author at Mercy Home Orphanage in Kampala, Uganda

Ephesians 4:29

Let no corrupt communication proceed out of your mouth, but that which is good to the use of edifying, that it may minister grace unto the hearers.

Chapter 4.

Turn It Around

Not on your own and not on the Lord's own, but together.

We must learn to speak in righteousness and order our speech. You need to ask the Lord to help you with that.

This is the prayer that was given to me that I use to accomplish this task.

Prayer

> Father God, in Jesus' name, I ask you to govern and order my speech today as well as the speech of my descendants and loved ones. Let every word be pleasing unto you. I ask you to intervene in this area and I give you permission and invite you to do so. In Jesus' name, Amen.

You cannot order your speech any more than you alone can order your steps. Your speech, without his help, will be flawed at best. You cannot control your tongue on your own, but at the same time you cannot just "roll it over on the Lord" thinking that he will just take care of it. I have seen many people that believe that and with little to no results. With his death upon the cross and his ascension into heaven, the subsequent dispensation of his Holy Spirit he has effectively "rolled it over on you." He has already been here once, and you have been given authority over all the power of the enemy. You must embrace that authority and use it. You are infinitely more powerful than you think. You are a child of the King; in fact, you are a king of the King and a priest of the Priest. Take your God-given authority, faith, and confidence and use them. Understand who you really are!

Remember when the Israelites left Egypt and came to the promised land? Did God go in there and wipe out the people that were currently occupying those lands? Did the Israelites just "roll it over on the Lord." To take care of it for them. No, he did not. He said he would *fight with them,* and they would be victorious. The same holds true for you and your words. You must make the effort to control your tongue and he will meet you there and together you will master your tongue. I know this to be a fact because I have lived it.

Luke 10:19 Behold I give unto you power to tread on scorpions and serpents, and over all the power of the enemy, and nothing shall by any means hurt you.

You must strive and work at controlling your speech and he will undoubtedly be with you, and you will gain much progress. Use the above prayer to invite Him into your efforts to control your tongue and keep working on it. You will see amazing results.

Confess, Repent, Renounce, and Recall Unholy Words

You must first confess the unholy words that you have spoken as sin.

Now repent for them and ask the Lord to forgive you for speaking them.

Renounce those words, take them back.

Recall all negative words. Assign the holy angels to go out into the universe and gather those words up in nets, bring them back and bury them at the feet of Jesus.

Ask the Lord to wash those unfortunate words away in the blood of His precious Son, Jesus Christ, never to be remembered against you again.

You will not have to give an account for those words at your final judgment because they do not even exist anymore. Even now.

May the Lord bless and keep you and yours.

Revelation 12:11

And they overcame him by the blood of the Lamb, and the word of their testimony: and they loved not their lives unto the death.

Colossians, 1:12-14

Giving thanks unto the Father, which has made us meet to be partakers of the inheritance of the saints in light. Who hath delivered us from the power of darkness, and hath translated us unto the Kingdom of His dear Son: In whom we have redemption through His blood, even the forgiveness of our sins.

Keep it Clean, Stay Repented.

Once you have cleansed yourself of inappropriate and negative or unholy words in your past, you now are clean and clear of all past sins of the tongue. Now you must "keep it clean" by repenting daily for any words that were spoken by you that were not right in the eyes of God. I usually do this every morning but there are times when I do not. I never let any more than a few days go by without washing those negative words away by the blood of his precious Son. Stay on top of it. The enemy will try to distract you from doing this because he knows how important it is. He will try to put you into a "spin," and he will put many things in front of you that you must take care of. You will say, "Well, I will just do this and that and then I will pray," *but there is always one more thing*!

A couple more things pop up and then a couple more until you missed your opportunity to pray. That is called an "unholy hindrance." When you see it, you bind all unholy hindrances from interfering in your prayer time. Please do not get *"caught up in the spin,"* now that you are aware of it.

Move Forward in the Grace that has been Given You.

You are in a unique position now with cleansed speech that is pleasing to the Lord. Be very conscious of every word that you speak. Weigh your words carefully. Be slow to speak and never just blurt anything out. Some people have a knack for probing others, they can bait you into saying things that you will regret later. Be aware of that and use your God-given discernment to see into the situations and people with which you must deal. See chapter 7. "The fear of the Lord."

The fear of the Lord is the beginning of wisdom. The first place it manifests itself is in the tongue. You can discern a person that has the fear of the

Lord through their speech. That is why I have included chapter 7 in this book. Without the fear of the Lord, it will be almost impossible to cleanse your tongue. If you want the Lord to help you with your words, I highly suggest that you choose to study this chapter. Ask the Holy Spirit to lead you into the fear of the Lord and he undoubtedly will. You will be miles and miles ahead of anyone else. Heads and shoulders above an ordinary person, you are certainly not just another person you are indeed a king of the King. So, move forward my friend in the grace that has been given you.

The people in the Body of Christ, enlightened, will look and sound entirely different than the people of the world.

The person with Godly understanding sees into the very nature of the people that they are dealing with or the very essence of the situation that they must handle. The fear of the Lord is the principal part of knowledge. Wisdom, understanding, and then knowledge.

Philippians 4:19

My God shall supply all my needs according to his riches in glory through Christ Jesus.

Luke 6:38

Give, and it shall be given unto you; in good measure, pressed down, running over, and shaken together; shall men give unto your bosom. For in the same measure that you mete withal, it shall be measured to you.

2nd Corinthians 9:8-10

And God is able to make all grace abound toward you; that ye, always having all sufficiency in all things, may abound to every good work:

As it is written, He hath dispersed abroad; he hath given to the poor; his righteousness remaineth forever.

Now he that ministereth seed to the sower both minister bread for your food, and multiply your seed sown, and increase the fruits of your righteousness.

The first place the fear of the Lord is manifested is in the tongue. Well-chosen words without exaggeration, profanity, or untruth, solemn words all pleasing to the Lord. Without idleness and foolishness, this marks the one who walks in the fear of the Lord. This fear leaves no compromise with evil. We are offered a good, long life, and many days that we may see good.

Speaking in Love

Philippians 4:8 Finally brethren, whatsoever things are true, whatsoever things are honest, whatsoever things are just, whatsoever things are pure, whatsoever things are lovely, whatsoever things are of good report; if there be any virtue, and if there be any praise, think on these things.

Ephesians 4:15 But speaking the truth in love, may grow up into him in all things, which is the head, even Christ.

Ephesians 4:25 Wherefore putting away lying, speak every man the truth with his neighbor; for we are members one of another.

Ephesians 4:29 let no corrupt communication proceed out of your mouth, but that which is good to the use of edifying, that it may minister grace unto the hearers.

1 Corinthians 13:13 NKJV And now abide faith, hope, love, these three; but the greatest of these is love.

Ephesians 5:4 Neither filthiness, nor foolish talking, nor jesting which are not convenient: but rather giving of thanks.

Colossians 3:8 But now ye also put off all these; anger, wrath, malice, blasphemy, and filthy communication out of your mouth.

1ˢᵗ Corinthians 13:4-8 ESV Love is patient and kind; love does not envy or boast; it is not arrogant or rude. It does not insist on its own way; it is not irritable or resentful. It does not rejoice at wrongdoing but rejoices with the truth. Love bears all things, believes all things, hopes all things, endures all things. Love never ends, as for prophecies they will pass away; as for tongues, they will cease; as for knowledge, it will pass away.

When you cast out the negative, unholy words you must replace them with something. That something is words of love, edification, exhortation, and comfort. Even when you must correct your children or somebody else, speak the truth in love. They may not like what they hear coming out of your mouth but if you say it in love they will be disarmed and hopefully understanding. Love is the greatest of all.

Intervene, Permission and Invite

These are immensely powerful words when used in prayer. They go together and it has been my experience that these words somehow will get the Creator's attention. *I have tried to use other words with basically the same meaning and have gotten nowhere!*

> **Now, I stick with what I know works, and this, dear saints does work, and it seems to work rather quickly.**

The first time I used these words in prayer was years ago. I did not expect to use them, I had no knowledge of their power. For some reason, I picked up a tablet and I wrote a general invitation for the Lord to intervene in my life and I gave Him permission to do so. This was on Christmas day.

Two days later my life changed dramatically. I know the Lord answered my prayer immediately. Keep in mind that what I asked for was a general intervention and that is exactly what I received. A life-changing far-reaching intervention that could only be described as miraculous.

I realized that if it worked so well in a general sense, it would probably work the same in a targeted application. I began to use these words in specific, targeted, well-defined areas of my life and I was very descriptive of what I needed intervention for, and I did receive it rather quickly. I have used that prayer many times now and there has not been one instance of not receiving or delay! That is definitely worth more than pure silver or fine gold. (see Isaiah 3:14).

Here is an example of a specific, targeted, well-defined prayer using those three powerful words:

Father God, I come to you this day *inviting* you to *intervene* in the problems I have been having with my finances. I give you *permission* to enter into this area of my life. It seems that no matter how much money I receive in a month, it all seems to be gone by the end of the month, if not sooner. I have not had success in saving money. I have tried many different strategies and all with little effect. I am not here this day to "roll it over on you, Lord." Because I understand that with your precious Son's death and resurrection and the gift of the Holy Spirit, you have effectively rolled it over on me.

I am here to ask you to intervene specifically in my finances, especially regarding a savings account. *I will be a "participant" and not a person that just sits back and waits for you to act.* I invite you into my finances and I give you permission to intervene. Give me the wisdom, knowledge, and courage to change my financial picture. Order my steps Lord, govern my life. Thank you, Father. I cover this entire situation in the impenetrable, shed, and resurrected blood of Jesus Christ, of Nazareth.

In Jesus' name, Amen.

I cover you, friends, with the impenetrable, shed and resurrected blood of Jesus Christ from the crowns of your heads to the soles of your feet.

James 1:26
If any man among you seem to be religious, and bridleth not his tongue, but deceiveth his own heart, this man's religion is vain.

Chapter 5.

Taming the Tongue

Taming the tongue

This small but immensely powerful part of the body must be held in check. Faith can do it. Faith acts wisely. Ask the Lord to bless the words of your mouth.

James, Chapter 1. Verse 26
If any man among you seem to be religious, and bridleth not his tongue, but deceiveth his own heart, this man's religion is vain.

James, Chapter 3.
My brethren, be not many masters, knowing that we shall receive the greater condemnation.

For in many things, we offend all. If any man offend not in word, the same is a perfect man, and able also to bridle the whole body.

Behold, we put bits in the horses' mouths, that they may obey us; and we turn about their whole body.

Behold also the ships, which though they be so great, and are driven of fierce winds, yet are they turned about with a very small helm, whithersoever the governor listeth.

Even so, the tongue is a little member, and boasteth great things. Behold, how great a matter a little fire kindleth!

And the tongue is a fire, a world of iniquity; so is the tongue among our members, that it defileth the whole body. And setteth on fire the course of nature; and it is set on fire of hell.

For every kind of beasts, and of birds, and of serpents, and of things in the sea, is tamed, and hath been tamed of mankind.

But the tongue can no man tame; it is an unruly evil full of deadly poison.

Therewith bless we God, even the Father; and therewith curse we men, which are made after the similitude of God.

Out of the same mouth proceedeth blessing and cursing. My brethren, these things ought not to be so.

Can the fig tree, my brethren, bear olive berries? Either a vine, figs? So can no fountain both yield salt water and fresh.

Who is a wise man and endued with knowledge among you let him shew out of a good conversation his works with meekness of wisdom.

But if ye have bitter envying and strife in your hearts, glory not, and lie not against the truth.

This wisdom descendeth not from above but is earthly, sensual, devilish.

For where envying and strife is, there is confusion and every evil work.

But the wisdom that is from above is first pure, then peaceable, gentle, and easy to be intreated, full of mercy and good fruits, without partiality, and without hypocrisy.

And the fruit of righteousness is sown in peace of them that make peace.

James, Chapter 4. Verses 11-12
Speak not evil one of another, brethren. He that speaketh evil of his brother, and judgeth his brother, speaketh evil of the law, and judgeth the law: but if thou judge the law, thou art not a doer of the law, but a judge.

Sins of the Tongue

Have you had problems with controlling your words? Have you prayed and prayed about it and just does not seem to be effective? There may be contamination in one or both of your bloodlines. Once I addressed this in my own life, I started to see that my words began to line up with the word of God. I became acutely aware of every word that I spoke, each and every day. (I have left you a prayer here, the one that God gave me to use, to keep aware and forgiven. It is also in the prayer section of this book.)

Prayer confess the sins of your tongue

Lord God, I confess the sins of my tongue over the past day. I confess all words that I spoke that were:

Words of idleness.
Words of foolishness.
Words without faith.
Words that were agreeing with the enemy.
All words that were blasphemous, profane, or untrue.
I confess all words that were unbecoming of me.
I confess all words that were disparaging to myself.
I confess all other words that were displeasing unto you.

I confess them as sin, and I repent of them. I now **renounce** every word that was not right, in your eyes, Lord.

I *recall* these words from floating through the universe and I send a detail of holy angels out to gather them up in nets and bring them back and bury them at the feet of Jesus.

I ask to be forgiven for these unfortunate words as I forgive myself for uttering them. I ask that they all be washed away by the blood of your precious Son, Jesus Christ never to be remembered against me again. And so that I will not be held accountable for these words at my final judgment, because… ***they do not even exist anymore***, even now.
Amen.

Be incredibly careful what words you use with your children. You, as their parents, have authority over them to bless them or curse them. Every time that you get angry with them, be careful of what you say to them. Never use disparaging words to them. You cannot say things like. "You are so dumb; how could you get a "D" in this subject?" "How dumb can you be?" and things along that line. I do not have to list them for you. You already know. Every time you use words like that to your children you are cursing them, and you were not even aware of it!

So, say things like "Well, I see you received a "D" in this subject, so now we know what we must work on. You are much smarter than that." Now praise them and tell them how blessed you are to have them for your child, how brilliant they are. That disparaging language towards your own children is damaging them, it must stop right away. Please do not disparage them with your language, speak to them in love, only say positive and encouraging words to them. You will receive the fruit thereof.

Be incredibly careful of the words that you use to describe yourself. Never use disparaging words, and negative words Like "That's just my luck." "This always happens to me." "I can't do anything right." Never use words that are "unbecoming" to the man or woman of God that you are. Speak like the child of God that you truly are. Watch your words so that absolutely none of them would be displeasing unto the Lord.

May healing and deliverance be yours.

Mathew 6:14,15

For if ye forgive men their trespasses, your heavenly Father will also forgive you:

But if you forgive not men their trespasses, neither will your Father forgive your trespasses.

Chapter 6.

Forgiveness Commanded

SCRIPTURES ON FORGIVENESS

Romans 12:17
Recompense to no man evil for evil. Provide things honest in the sight of all men.

Ephesians 4:31,32
Let all bitterness, and wrath, and anger, and clamour, and evil speaking, be put away from you, with all malice. And be he kind to one another, tenderhearted, forgiving one another even as God for Christ's sake hath forgiven you.

Daniel 9:9
To the Lord, our God belong mercies and forgiveness, though we have rebelled against him.

Luke 6:27
But I say unto you which hear, love your enemies, be good to them which hate you.

Luke 6:37
Judge not, and ye shall not be judged: condemn not, and ye shall not be condemned: forgive and ye shall be forgiven.

Numbers 14:18
The Lord is longsuffering, and of great mercy, forgiving iniquity and transgression and by no means clearing the guilty, visiting the iniquity of the fathers upon the children unto the third and fourth generation.

Mark 11:25
And when you stand praying, forgive, if ye have ought against any: that your Father which is in heaven may forgive you your trespasses.

Isaiah 43:25
I, even I, am he that blotteth out thy transgression for mine own sake, and will not remember thy sins.

Psalm 32:1
Blessed is he whose transgression is forgiven, whose sin is covered

You are commanded to forgive

When you stand praying, forgive, if ye have ought against any: That your Father also which is in heaven may forgive you your trespasses. But if ye do not forgive, neither will your Father which is in heaven forgive your trespasses. (Mark 11:25-26.) These are the words of Jesus. Without forgiveness, your efforts to tame your tongue will fall short.

To Confess, repent, renounce, and recall your ungodly words is what this book is about, but there is another equally important aspect of this cleansing and that is forgiveness. You must forgive all who have trespassed against you for speaking negatively into your life, as well as the lives of your descendants and loved ones. This includes your ancestors, parents, doctors, teachers, and supervisors as well as your friends and acquaintances, and especially yourself.

Those that have or had the authority over you also had the ability to put into place word curses that are extremely damaging. However, the words that you yourself have spoken over yourself are the most powerful witness against you.

To move forward, you are going to have to fully forgive all the people that have spoken negatively about you or into your life. All of them who were or are in authority over you, that have done so. and to end this, you are going to have to forgive yourself.

Those that are Related or Close to You.

Your family
Your ancestors
Your husband or wife
Friends and acquaintances
Yourself

Those who were or are in Authority Over You.

Your parents
Your supervisors at work
Your teachers
Medical professionals
The authorities

Your landlord
Your debtors

The Prayer of Forgiveness

I stand before you this day to forgive all who have trespassed against me and mine by speaking disparaging and denigrating words into our lives. Whether they be slander or lies. Whether they be truth or a mixture thereof.

As an act of my will, I choose to forgive every one of them by the grace that I have been given just as you, Father forgave me. I realize that I am giving them a gift that they do not deserve, just as I did not. I forgive them all.

I also ask that you forgive them for sinning against you for I know that first and foremost their words were against you, before me.

Finally, I ask that you forgive me for the things that I have said about myself, my children, my family, and all others. For I know that my unholy words far outweigh the words of others and have the power to cause the most damage.

I now break the power of those word curses against me and mine by the authority that I have to invoke the name of Jesus Christ.

I break off each and every word curse that has been spoken over me and mine by my ancestors, friends, and family or by those who are or were in authority over me, and I forgive these people for negatively speaking into my life. In Jesus' name, Amen.

To thoroughly break off these curses, you are going to have to spend some time in prayer with the Lord. Ask Him to show you what has been placed upon you. I did this by bringing up each person to the Lord, one by one, who may have spoken into my life negatively. I did this each morning during my prayer time until it was a completed work.

As I did this, I noticed that the Lord met me there and granted me the wisdom and knowledge to proceed in this endeavor. I did not know that I was finished with this until one morning there was just nothing more left to bring to the Lord.

This was a big part of my life for a season, but now it had finally ended, and I was able to move on. This is the only way that you can thoroughly remove all the word curses from your life. Once again, I must tell you, brothers, and sisters, to just pray "I break off all the word curses that have ever been spoken against me." will simply not cut it.

Remember, these word curses for the most part were placed upon you and yours through the ignorance of the speakers, and not in malice. And that you have also spoken word curses into the lives of others through ignorance and you must repent for doing so and ask forgiveness for yourself. Refrain from any words that disparage others. Can you see the enormous damage that negative words cause?

The key is to repent, renounce those words, recall them and refrain from ever using words like that again.

The people who have spoken negatively into your lives must be forgiven, one by one.

Forgive and you shall be forgiven.

Job 28:28

And unto man he said, Behold the fear of the Lord, that is wisdom, and to depart from evil is understanding.

Chapter 7.

The Fear of the Lord

Scriptures

Job 28:20-28. Whence then cometh wisdom? And where is the place of understanding?

Seeing it is hid from the eyes of all living. And kept close from the fowls of the air.

Destruction and death say We have heard the fame thereof with our ears.

God understandeth the way thereof, and he knoweth the place thereof.

For he looketh to the ends of the earth and seeth under the whole heaven.

To make the weight for the winds, and he weigheth the waters by measure.

When he made a decree for the rain. And a way for the lightning of the thunder.

Then did he see it, and declare it; he prepared it, yea, and searched it out.

And unto man he said, Behold, the fear of the Lord, that is wisdom; and to depart from evil is understanding.

The fear of the Lord is obedience to the first commandment. (Exodus 20:3). Giving God his rightful place.

Isaiah 11:1-3. There shall come forth a rod from the stem of Jesse (that is Jesus) and a branch shall grow out of his roots. The Spirit of the Lord shall rest upon him. The spirit of wisdom and understanding. The spirit of counsel and might, the spirit of knowledge and of the fear of The Lord.

And shall make him of quick understanding in the fear of the Lord: and he shall not judge by the sight of his eyes, neither reprove after the hearing of his ears.

Proverbs 19:23. The fear of the Lord tendeth to life and he that hath it shall abide satisfied; he shall not be visited with evil.

Proverbs 22:4. By humility, and the fear of the Lord are riches, honor, and life.

Proverbs 23:17,18. Let not thine heart envy sinners; but be thou in the fear of the Lord all the day long.

For surely there is an end and thine expectation shall not be cut off.

Revelation 4:5. And out of the throne proceeded lightning, thundering, and voices. And there were seven lamps of fire burning before the throne, which are the seven Spirits of God.

Proverbs 14:26,27. In The fear of the Lord is strong confidence: and his children shall have a place of refuge. The fear of the Lord is a fountain of life, to depart from the snares of death.

Jeremiah 17:7-8 Blessed is the man who trusts in the Lord, whose hope the Lord is. For He shall be as a tree planted by the waters, and that spreadeth out her roots by the river, and shall not see when heat cometh, but her leaf shall be green; and shall not be careful in the year of drought, neither shall cease from bearing fruit.

Jeremiah 17:5-8. Thus, saith the Lord; Cursed be the man, who trusts in man, who depends on flesh for strength and maketh flesh his arm, and whose heart departeth from the Lord. For he shall be like the heath in the desert and shall not see when good cometh; but shall inhabit the parched places in the wilderness, in a salt land and not inhabited.

Proverbs 8:13 The Fear of the Lord is to hate evil: pride, and arrogancy, and the evil way, and the froward mouth, do I hate.

Proverbs 1:20-33 Wisdom crieth without; she uttereth her voice in the streets; she crieth in the chief place of concourse, in the opening of the gate; in the city she uttereth her words saying, how long, ye simple ones, will ye love simplicity? And the scorners delight in their scorning and fools hate knowledge? Turn you at my reproof: behold I will pour out my Spirit unto you, I will make known my words unto you. Because I have called, and ye refused; I have stretched out my hand, and no man regarded; but ye have set at naught all my counsel and would none of my reproof: I also will laugh at your calamity; I will mock when your fear cometh; when your fear cometh as desolation, and your destruction cometh as a whirlwind; when distress and anguish cometh upon you. Then shall they call upon me, but I will not answer; they shall seek me early, but they shall not find me; for that they hated knowledge and did not choose the fear of the Lord: they would none of my counsel: they despised all my reproof. Therefore, shall they eat of the fruit of their own way, and be filled with their own devices. For the turning away of the simple shall slay them, and the prosperity of fools shall destroy them. But whoso hearkeneth unto me shall dwell safely and shall be quiet from fear of evil.

> *"Conduct yourselves through the time of your sojourning here, in fear." This is addressed to God's redeemed people.*

We are all going to have to give an account of ourselves and the price that God was willing to pay for our redemption. The most precious thing in the universe was paid for our redemption. That should cause us to live in the reverent fear of the Lord.

To Depart from Evil is Understanding.

Behold, the fear of the Lord, that is wisdom. And to depart from evil, is understanding. If you want access to that wisdom, the only way that you can attain it is through the fear of the Lord. True wisdom is through the fear of the Lord and living a life of righteousness.

> *Wisdom is the Primary Thing, then Understanding, and then Knowledge.*

Wisdom is the primary thing and out of it proceeds understanding. Understanding means insight into the *real* nature of people and situations. It is much more than smarts. A bright person can be easily fooled, not so with the one that remains in the fear of the Lord.

But the person with Godly understanding sees into the very nature of the people that they are dealing with, and the situations that they must manage. The fear of the Lord is the principal part of knowledge.

Wisdom, understanding, and then knowledge.

I believe this has been mostly neglected in the church today. Something overlooked. The fear of the Lord is the fountain of life.

The secret of the Lord is with those who fear Him. The man who keeps the first commandment by putting nothing else ahead of, or on par with God has the fear of the Lord.

The key to wisdom is in the fear of the Lord. To continue in the fear of the Lord will bring about your perfection.

All-encompassing blessings and prosperity are promised to those who fear the Lord.

Distress and Anguish are Reserved for Those who do not fear Him.

Without the fear of the Lord, you have already rejected God's blessing. I believe that without it you can block your prosperity even if you tithe and keep everything else. If you think that tithing alone is going to further your prosperity, you are mistaken. I have seen many people, over the years, who tithed and tithed and never got anywhere at all. You simply cannot stand on one principle and ignore the rest. *The beginning of wisdom* is the fear of the Lord. So, start there, saints.

> *You need to pursue it. It is a definite personal choice. Choose the fear of the Lord and ask the Holy Spirit to help you receive it.*

He set aside his own will in favor of the Father's will, as we should also do. Jesus's prayers were always answered (as a man and not God.) The fear of the Lord led Him *to always pray the Father's will.* (Isaiah 11:1-3). If Jesus, the sinless Son of God needed the fear of the Lord, then how much more do you and I stand in need.

A Personal Testimony

Before I acquired the fear of the Lord, when I was young, I took people and situations at face value. If people were friendly and nice, smiled at me, or patted me on the back, I would assume their intentions were good. I had no discernment or insight into the real nature of people or situations. Now, I can see deeply into these things. I know when somebody has bad intentions or if a person or situation needs to be avoided, and I recognize those who seek to use me. Since I do not have those tendencies myself, they are very foreign to me. I have also found out that those kinds of people are rarely taken advantage of because they see the same discoloration that is in them, in those that seek to exploit them.

If you think you can go through life without the fear of the Lord, you will fall into one snare after another. This does not only affect you, but it also impacts your family and friends as well. The fear of the Lord is most definitely the beginning of wisdom.

I recall the first house that I bought when I was still a young man. The realtor was very friendly and accommodating. He *seemed* to have my interests at heart. He was also the agent for the sellers. He had what they call a "dual agency." Everything went along smoothly until one afternoon

I received a call at work from the realtor. He said that he was at the title company and there was a big problem and asked if I would come over there immediately.

When I arrived, he was in an office with the sellers. They all had big frowns on their faces and looked distraught. I asked what is the problem to which he replied. "The lender is having problems getting you financed because you simply do not make enough money to qualify for the loan," I replied "Well, they did not seem to have a problem before, why now, at the last minute?" He said he did not know. He kept asking me if I could ask for a raise or borrow money from somebody to put it into the down payment. I told him there was no way. He said, "Well, we do have a fix for this, but we did not want to use it unless it was absolutely necessary."

The "fix" they came up with was that the sellers would loan me $6,000.00 (at a substantial interest rate.) to be paid back in monthly installments. The sellers told me that they did not want to loan me that money, but that they did want to sell the house because they are moving, and this throws a monkey wrench into their plans. I agreed to do it because I thought it was a legitimate transaction. I remember thanking them profusely for their generosity.

The house closed and I moved in, my installment payments to the sellers were to begin shortly. I started thinking over everything and I pulled out the contract and read it quite thoroughly and there was no record of a $6,000.00 transaction in the closing documents. I began to realize that these people tried to scam me. I thought why would they want to do that? I was young and trying to buy my first house and they, including the realtor, were older, well-established, and financially secure individuals. So, I thought if they already "have it all, why take advantage of me?" The answer is; *because they will do what they can. No matter how old they are or how rich they are.* Especially the rich, there is something in them that propels them to take advantage of the poor. I have seen this hundreds of times in my life and in the lives of others. Do not be deceived.

I did not pay my first installment to the sellers, a couple of weeks later they called, and I made up some excuse. Two weeks later the realtor called and seemed so hurt that after "all they did for you," you have not even made your first payment. After that, I never heard from any of them ever again. They, having realized that I figured them out, just gave up and moved on.

If I would have had the fear of the Lord at the time, I would have been able to *see right through them!* I lived years without the fear of the Lord because I simply did not know about it. I went to church and of all the sermons I heard I never once heard anything about the fear of the Lord. Yet it is of vital importance. If you have not received it, ask the Holy Spirit to lead you into it, I highly suggest that you do so now. I also suggest that you look up the scriptures introduced in this chapter, read them over yourself, and meditate on them. You will realize the magnitude of this teaching. The Holy Spirit will teach you the fear of the Lord. It must be taught. If you are not willing to be taught, or if you have an unwilling attitude or are unteachable, you will never master the fear of the Lord. How can you master that which has never been brought to and explained to you? This teaching and these scriptures should cause you to want to "dig it out." I sincerely pray that you will receive this.

The Fear of the Lord is Manifested in your Words.

The first place the fear of the Lord is manifested is in the tongue. Well-chosen words without exaggeration, solemn words all pleasing to the Lord, without idleness and foolishness, without profanity. This marks the speech of the one who walks in the fear of the Lord. The fear of the Lord will lead you to obedience even to the point of suffering. Jesus, even though he was a

Son, He learned obedience through suffering. You also learned obedience through suffering and so do your children, and so do your animals and pets.

The fear of the Lord will deliver you from all other kinds of fear, you will no longer have to deal with anxiety and worry, fearing what will happen next. God's children will have a place of refuge and security. It will keep you from the snares of death and impart to you strong confidence. The fear of the Lord is a fountain of life. This is all promised in Proverbs 14:26-27. This my friends is the source of life, and it will permeate your lives and lifestyle.

> **The people in the Body of Christ, enlightened, will look and sound entirely different than the people of the world.**

One example of a fear that I have noticed in people is the fear of what others will think or say. People that are after self-promotion, and out to "garner a following," or to obtain wealth. Also, those that pursue pleasure and have no time to study teaching such as this. People like this are unstable and undependable, even double-minded. I have found that you cannot trust them. they do not make good friends or spouses. They do not exhibit the fear of the Lord.

The Fear of the Lord

Psalms 19:9-14. The fear of the Lord is clean, enduring forever: the judgments of the Lord are true and righteous altogether. More to be desired are they than gold, yea, than much fine gold: sweeter also than honey and the honeycomb.

*Moreover, by them is thy servant warned: ***

And in the keeping of them, there is great reward. Who can understand his errors? Cleanse thou me from secret faults. Keep back thy servant also from presumptuous sins; let them not have dominion over me: then shall I be upright, and I shall be innocent from the great transgression. Let the words of my mouth, and the meditation of my heart, be acceptable in thy sight, O Lord, my strength, and my redeemer.

> *Do you understand the significance of and the far-reaching benefits of being able to be warned? Warned about other people and situations, warned about your children, warned about the conditions and the times. Warned about your diet and the health of you and yours?... **To be given a warning by the Lord Himself** about anything that affects you and yours comes with the fear of the Lord!

(Proverbs 2:1-5). My son, if thou wilt receive my words, and hide my commandments with thee; so that thou incline thine ear unto wisdom, and apply thine heart to understanding; yea, if thou criest after knowledge, and liftest up thy voice for understanding; If thou seekest her as silver and searchest for her as for hid treasures; then shalt thou understand the fear of the Lord and find the knowledge of God.

Cry out to God in prayer, lift your voice up to Him, and search for wisdom. Do not be the one who did not answer wisdom's call because when you finally do cry out to her, in your need, she will not answer. You must seek, and search for it. Jesus spoke a parable about treasure in a field. He said the man who wanted the treasure had to buy the field. So first, there is a price. Then he had to search in the field for where the treasure was. When he found where the treasure was, he had to dig it out.

Sin is a reproach to any nation, and it is also a reproach to you personally.

Know this; your sins will raise up and empower enemies and adversaries against you!

Fear the Lord and Him only. Refrain from all sin to be counted a child of God. The true child of God will still have enemies and adversaries, but they will not be (*raised up and empowered against you.*)

I have learned obedience to the Lord through suffering, and I have learned to *fear Him*. I pray that you will receive this teaching.

The fear of the Lord?
Destruction and death say **WE** have heard the fame thereof.

Proverbs 26:2
As the bird by wandering, as the swallow by flying, So, the curse, causeless shall not come

Chapter 8.

WORD CURSES

Your Word Curses

Word curses are unholy words that you have spoken over yourself of which you probably were unaware. This also holds true for the words that you have spoken over your children and others in ignorance. Hopefully not maliciously.

You can receive word curses from the negative words spoken to you by your parents, your teachers, and your supervisors or anyone that is or has been in authority over you, such as at work or even from a teacher or doctor. If you are in authority over others you can deliver, into their lives, curses, by your careless words. *Be aware of this.* It is my sincere desire to make you aware of the power of these words to curse, and of course to turn it around by equipping you to use your words to bless, to speak in love, and to speak words that are pleasing to God. Let us start with the words that you have used that are contrary to your own personal wellbeing.

Word Curses that you have Inadvertently Placed upon Yourself

These are mostly word curses that you have spoken that are in opposition to the will of God for you, and that are harming you. You above anyone else on Earth have the power to both bless and curse yourself. Every time you utter negative things about yourself, to yourself or others, regarding yourself, you are in effect cursing yourself. You are empowering this negativity to become a reality in your own life.

You cannot even blame Satan for that because that is YOUR TESTIMONY OF YOURSELF. This must be stopped immediately. Realize that there is power in your words, both positive and negative. You are made in the image of God, and he framed the entire universe with his words. One of the most powerful gifts that you have is the ability to use words, so begin to be very aware of what you say from this day on.

For example, if you say things like; "I'm always broke, I can't seem to save a dime." "Well, that's just my luck." or "This always happens to me." The "eavesdropping Demons" just heard that, and they go to work to make that statement FROM YOUR very OWN MOUTH a lifelong reality. Realize this; unless you repent for that statement and all others that are not right in the eyes of God you may live that out. I have lived through it, and I have seen many hundreds of others that have eaten the fruit of their very own tongues. Trust me on this one.

I remember my uncle, every time we went to visit him and my aunt, he was always complaining about being a "pauper." I asked my dad "What is a pauper?" I found out that it is someone who is broke. He complained about not having enough money all the time. He was obsessed with his "poverty lifestyle." and how he just could not get ahead, and he voiced it repeatedly. I was just a kid, but I sure noticed his whining and moaning over a lack of money constantly.

As I grew older, I saw that the house they lived in was extremely valuable property. I also knew they had a farm in another state that was quite a prize. Here he was groaning over his lack when he was worth well over two million dollars and he didn't even know it! In fact, after his death, they sold "that old worthless farm." for an even million dollars, but he did not see any of that money because he died in his mid-fifties, broke, or so he thought and spoke. Remember, as a man thinketh in his heart, SO IS HE.

So, cease all denigrating and disparaging words and phrases about yourself, or they will undoubtedly be conducted, very painfully over your entire lifetime. You certainly do not need that and neither do your children and grandchildren.

On the opposite side, start to use words that will bless you. You need to start looking at yourself the way that God sees you. He sees you through Jesus as complete, lacking nothing.

Word Curses from Those Who are or were in Authority Over You.

You do not have to receive negative words spoken to you from a person or persons that are in or were in authority over you. When I hear words spoken to me that clearly are in violation of me, I simply say to myself, "I do not receive that in Jesus' name."

Those in authority over us have the power to invoke word curses upon us. In most cases, this is due to their ignorance. Your parents may not have known that every word they spoke to you that was not right in the eyes of God, had the potential to become a *LIFELONG CURSE* to you because they had both the power to bless and to curse their very own children. I grew up under many word curses spoken by my very own parents, not out of malice but out of ignorance. So did almost everyone else that I knew, and their own parents did the same thing to them. This is a perpetuating problem passed down through the generations that you have the power to put a stop to right now. Look and ponder the destruction that these word curses have had upon their children! In most cases, I have found that this problem is absent in Jewish households.

I had to go back in prayer to the Lord and root out all those word curses and repent **for my parents** for saying them to me, and to repent for any that I unknowingly said to my children and grandchildren. I wrote out my blessings to them and gave them to them. I want to make you aware of the dangers of using improper words with your children. You will shape their lives one way or the other.

Other sources of word curses can come from teachers, bosses or supervisors, doctors, or just anyone else in authority. Now when I hear anything like that my ears perk up for I am keenly aware of the dangers of word curses, and you will be too.

Sins of the Tongue

Have you had problems with controlling your words? Have you prayed and prayed about it and it does not seem to make much difference? There may be contamination in one or both of your bloodlines. Once I addressed this in my own life, I started to see that my words began to line up with the word of God. I became acutely aware of every word that I spoke, every day. Consult chapter 9. "Confess the sins of your tongue."

Be incredibly careful what words you use with your children. You, as their parents have authority over them to bless them or to curse them. Every time that you get angry with them, be careful of what you say to them. Never use disparaging words to them. You cannot say things like, "Your so dumb, how could you get a "D" in this subject?" "How dumb can you be?" and things along that line. I do not have to list them for you. You already know. Every time you use words like that to your children you are cursing them, and you were not even aware of it! So, say things like; "Well, I see you received a "D" in this subject, so now we know what we must work on. You are much smarter than that." Now praise them and tell them how blessed you are to have them for your child, speak to them in love and, tell them how brilliant they are. You get the picture, don't you? That disparaging language towards your own children is damaging them, it must stop right away.

Proverbs 22:6. *Train up a child in the way he should go and when he is old he will not depart from it.*

Never agree with the enemy. Other people, although innocently, will sometimes say things to you that you should not agree to. I have found this to be a subtle snare in my life. I had a doctor tell me one time "Well, you know you have this disease, and it's eventually going to kill you." I said, "Yes I know but I'm doing the best I can." By the time I got out into the parking lot, I was convicted of agreeing with the enemy. (not that the doctor was an enemy.) I had to start repenting for that right away. What a horrible thing for me to agree to! As it turned out, upon further testing by a different doctor, I did not even have that disease! I did not find that out for over two years. Do not ever agree with anyone that goes against the knowledge of the most-high God.

Be aware of your words. Repent for any words that are not right in the Father's eyes. Renounce those words. Recall those words, ask the holy angels to go out and gather them up and bring them back and bury them at the feet of Jesus. Repent for the words of your ancestors on both sides. Ask the Lord to show you the transgressions in their spoken words. He will start opening up to you about what you are genetically made of. Now forgive all others who have spoken words to you that were not correct in the Father's eyes, especially those who were or are in authority over you such as parents, teachers, supervisors, and the like. This will take time because you have undoubtedly endured many instances of ill-spoken words by many people, we all have. This must be worked through. This is taken from my book "Holy Blood Transfusion." If you do not have a copy, I highly recommend that you obtain one.

Father God, anoint me with your Holy Spirit
Mark me with your Holy Name
Pour your Holy Oil upon my head
Put your Holy Words in my mouth

Chapter 9.

PRAYERS

Give thanks for those that have held you up and interceded for you and yours when you could not do it for yourself.

My voice shall you hear in the morning, O Lord; in the morning will I direct my prayer unto thee and look up. (Psalms 5:3)

Now, more than ever, we must *stay in an attitude of prayer* the entire day. We cannot just carve out a piece of time here and there for the Lord. Even our early morning prayer times are not enough. We cannot assume that just by attending church every Sunday will, by itself, be enough for us.

Prayers

Take your Hands off God's Property

Devil, I demand and command that you take your hands off God's property. I am a blood-bought child of the King and I rebuke and bind you and your evil, wicked, and demonic servants from interfering with the words of my mouth.

By the authority that I have been given to invoke the name of Jesus Christ, I cast you devils, demons, wicked, corrupt, and evil spirits into the pit, and I seal you in there with the blood of Christ. Go, get out! Be gone in Jesus' name.

I now loose the opposite spirits from heaven into my life today. I loose the seven-fold Spirit of the Lord and Holy Spirit.

Amen.

Father, Order my Speech

Father, in Jesus' name, I ask you to govern and order my speech today as well as the speech of my loved ones and descendants. Let every word be pleasing unto you. I ask you to intervene in this area and I give you permission and invite you to do so. In Jesus' name, Amen.

Faithful, Available, and Teachable

Here am I Lord, I am faithful, available, teachable, and thankful. I am here to worship you, praise you, and thank you for all that you have done, and for all you have given me. I thank you for all I have ever been and for all I am now, and for all I ever will be. *I seek to minister to you, Lord,* through praise and worship.

I want to bless you with my praise and worship because I can and because I want to and because you love to hear from me each and every morning. I desire to talk to you in the morning and tell you everything that is on my heart. I know I can trust you. "Blessed is the man who trusts in the Lord and whose hope the lord is." Jeremiah 17:7.

If there is anything that you want to tell me, show me, or just press into me, I am willing. If there is any place you want to take me to, I am ready. If there is any other supernatural form of communication that I am not aware of, that you want to use, I am available, stepping forward and not backward. Amen.

Binding Eavesdropping Spirits

Lord Jesus, I thank you for taking me off the enemy's radar and off his frequency. I ask you to scramble my words today to you in prayer, as well as my words to myself or to anyone else, both oral and written so that the enemy cannot eavesdrop on me and understand any of my communication.

I now bind the enemy's eavesdropping spirits, those assigned to me and mine today. I bind you spirits now in the name of Jesus Christ, and cast you into the pit. I seal you in there with the blood of Christ.

I now loose the opposite spirits from Heaven into my life today and the seven-fold spirit of the Lord and the Holy Spirit, instead. Thank you, Lord Jesus, Amen.

Setting the Atmosphere

To set the atmosphere for your prayer time, you must clean and clear all negative spiritual forces from your place of prayer.

Lord Jesus, I pray that if there be any spirits in this house/place that are devils, demons or wicked corrupt and evil, now I am talking to you, devils. I break your power in the name of Jesus Christ and I cast you into the pit and I seal you in there with the blood of Christ. Go, get out, disperse now! If there are any other spirits in this place that just do not belong here, I give you leave now and send you to the feet of Jesus for Him to do with you as he will. Go, move it. Be gone!

I now loose the holy angels, the seven-fold Spirit of the Lord, and the Holy Spirit into this place to replace what I have just cast out. Welcome Holy Spirit, come and permeate the atmosphere. magnificent Father of mercy and grace you are welcome in this place. Amen.

Submitting Your Will to the Lord

I submit my will, my rights, and all control to you today, Lord. I ask you to intervene and I give you permission and an invitation to order my steps and govern my life today in the name of Jesus Christ.

Father, I bind all thrones and dominions of darkness, all rulers and authorities, all powers and principalities, all spiritual wickedness in high places.

I bind all traveling demons, all lifestyle demons, all territorial demons.

I bind the ancestral and familiar spirit demons which are tied to the names of _____. and _____. (Mother and father's last names.)

I bind you all now by the authority that I have, to use the name of Jesus Christ and to apply his blood. Go! devils, get out! I cast you into the pit in the name of Jesus and I seal you in there with his blood.

Heavenly Father, I now loose the holy angels into my life today, instead. I loose the seven-fold Spirit of the Lord, the spirit of wisdom and understanding, the spirit of counsel and might, the spirit of knowledge, and the fear of the Lord. Holy Spirit, you are welcome in my life today. Come and lead me into all truth. Help me and comfort me. Be with me in a mighty way.

Amen.

The Whole Armor of God

Ephesians 6:10-18
Finally, my brethren, be strong in the Lord and in the power of his might. Put on the whole armor of God that you may be able to stand against all the wiles of the Devil.

For we wrestle not against flesh and blood, but against principalities, against powers, against the rulers of the darkness of this world, against spiritual wickedness in high places.

Therefore, take unto you the whole armor of God, that ye may be able to withstand in the evil day, and having done all to stand, stand therefore having your loins gird about with truth, having on the breastplate of righteousness and your feet shod with the preparation of the gospel of peace.

Above all taking the shield of faith wherewith ye shall be able to quench all the fiery darts of the wicked and take the helmet of salvation and the sword of the spirit which is the word of God. Praying always with all prayer and supplication for all the saints. Amen.

The Impenetrable Hedge of Protection

Lord, I thank you for my giftings, and anointings and for holding me up so that I in turn will be able to hold up the people that have been assigned to me.

Lord, I thank you for the impenetrable hedge of protection that you have kept up around me for quite some time now and I ask that you place that hedge around me again today for I have need of it.

An impenetrable hedge of protection to protect me from the attacks of the evil, wicked, and demonic spirits, the more recently departed lost, wandering souls, the spiritual wickedness in high places, and the wicked people.

I thank you, Lord Jesus, Amen.

Covering Our Loved Ones and Descendants

By the authority that I have to invoke the name of Jesus Christ, I rebuke and bind you devils and demons and you wicked, corrupt, and evil spirits, you that have been assigned to array around me and mine today. As a king of the King, I declare that your assignments are broken, canceled, fruitless, null and void and of none effect. I now cast you into the pit and I seal you in there with the blood of Christ.

Now I loose the opposite spirits from heaven into our lives today instead. And I loose the Holy Spirit and the seven-fold spirit of the Lord.

I cover myself and my entire line of descendants and loved ones with the impenetrable, shed, and resurrected blood of Jesus Christ from the crowns of our heads to the soles of our feet, so that no harm may penetrate, in Jesus' name I pray.

Amen.

Breaking off Curses

Heavenly Father, I silence and bind any, and all curses that have been or will be cast at me or any of my descendants or loved ones today (or over the past few days.) I break the power of this witchcraft now! I do this by the authority that I have, to invoke the name of Jesus Christ and to apply his blood. As a king of the King and a priest of the Priest I declare and decree that all this witchcraft is canceled, fruitless, null and void, and of none effect. Father, I renounce and break off any, and all:

Curses
Spells
Hexes
Vexes
Bewitchments
Jinxes
Hoodoo
Voodoo
Incantations
Enchantments
Satanic singing, chanting, rituals, isolation, and the spin.

I break off the curses of:
Disappointment
Frustration
Futility
Damage
Hurt
Pain
Suffering
Sorrow
Misery
Death

I break off the curses of:
Confusion
Confoundedness
Consternation
Mind fog

Mind blinding
Mind control
Mind hindering and blocking
Mind scattering and wandering

And any, and all other mind control curses, even those that I may not be aware of at this time.

I break off the curses of not being able to see what I need to see, find what I need to find, get what I need to get, comprehend what I need to comprehend, and meet who I need to meet.

I break off the curses of:
Fear
Rejection
Torment
Affliction
Damnation
Sadness
Despair
Negative thinking
Hopelessness
Anxiety
Depression
Repression
The oppression of the enemy.

I break off the curses of all manner of bondage and mental illness.

I break off the curses of automatic failure, relational difficulties, and familiar alienation.

I break off the curses of being my own worst enemy, everything I touch turns to dung. All my efforts being in vain and all my good intentions going sour.

I break off the curses of financial damnation, poverty, and lack.

I break off the curses of sickness and disease and poor health.

I break off the curses of bitterness and resentment isolation and loneliness, humiliation, and defeat.

I break off the curses of losing:
Losing gained ground
Losing contests
Competitions
Court cases
Losing family and friends
Losing money, valuables, property, and assets.
Losing jobs, joy, peace, happiness, and good health.
Losing respect and influence
Time and opportunities

And any other blessings and commodities that I certainly would not want to lose, even though I may not be aware of them at this time.

I renounce and break off all these curses and any others that I am not aware of, including the unspoken curses, the unknown curses, and the hidden curses. I break their power and Father, I reverse these curses back upon the heads of those servants of Satan who have cast them at me, seven-fold, (Psalm 109:17-20).

In order to attack the kingdom of darkness and his servants and to rend them, stop them, disable them, scatter them, humiliate, and defeat them. May they realize that by cursing me they are only cursing themselves. I return all their evil words, actions, and deeds back upon their own heads seven-fold. I ask you, Father, to rebuke the enemies of my very soul. I ask you to deliver a Holy Vengeance and righteous retribution to them that hate me and mine. This I pray in Jesus' name.

If any of these people, that have cast curses at me and mine, are appointed unto salvation, I cover them with the blood of Christ and with love and forgiveness, I thank you Lord for saving them, and I richly bless them in your Holy Name.

If they are not to receive salvation, I request that you wither them like the fig tree, dry them up and blow them away with your Holy Breath. (Exodus 22:18 Suffer not a witch to live.) Nevertheless, Father, not my will but… **may your will be done.**

Lord, God I replace these curses with your blessings. I call them forth in direct opposition to the curses that I have just broken. I call forth the unspoken blessings, the unknown blessings, and the hidden blessings. May your blessings shower down upon us from the open windows of heaven like a multitude of shimmering diamonds into the house of _____ and _____. May I/we be blessed in proportion to the cursing that I/we have endured. In Jesus' name, Amen.

Breaking Free Prayer

Lord Jesus, I thank you for the ministry of healing, deliverance, and intercession.

I realize that the sickness and evil that I have encountered today is more than my humanity can bear.

I ask you to cleanse me of anything negative that I may have picked up while interceding for myself, and others, and for binding the powers of darkness.

If any evil spirits have attempted to attach themselves to me or oppress me in any way, I address them now, you evil spirits, I break your power and I cast you into the pit and I seal you in there with the blood of Christ.

As a king of the King and a priest of the Priest, I decree that there will be no backlash, retribution, revenge, or spiritual retaliation leveled at me because of the prayers that I have offered up this day.

I thank you, Jesus, Amen.

The Prayer of Forgiveness

I stand before you this day to forgive all who have trespassed against me and mine by speaking disparaging and denigrating words into our lives. Whether they be slander or lies, whether they be truth or a mixture thereof.

As an act of my will, I choose to forgive every one of them by the grace that I have been given just as you, Father, forgave me. I realize that I am giving them a gift that they do not deserve, just as I did not. I forgive them all.

I also ask that you forgive them for sinning against you for I know that first and foremost their words were against you, before me.

Finally, I ask that you forgive me for the things that I have said about myself, my children, my family, and all others. For I know that my unholy words far outweigh the words of others. In Jesus' name, Amen.

Confess the Sins of Your Tongue

Lord God, I confess the sins of my tongue over the past day. I confess all words that I spoke that were:

Words of idleness.
Words of foolishness.
Words without faith.
Words that were agreeing with the enemy.
All words that were blasphemous, profane, or untrue.
I confess all words that were unbecoming of me.
I confess all words that were disparaging to myself.
I confess all other words that were displeasing unto you.

I confess them as sin, and I repent of them. I now **renounce** every word that was not right, in your eyes, Lord.

I **recall** these words from floating through the universe and I send a detail of holy angels out to gather them up in nets and bring them back and bury them at the feet of Jesus.

I ask to be forgiven for these unfortunate words as I forgive myself for uttering them. I ask that they all be washed away by the blood of your

precious Son, Jesus Christ never to be remembered against me again. And so that I will not be held accountable for these words at my final judgment, because… **they do not even exist anymore**, even now.
Amen.

Binding and Loosing

Whenever you bind and cast something out, you must replace it with the opposite spirit from Heaven. "I loose into those swept clean places the opposite spirits from Heaven, and the seven-fold Spirit of the Lord; the spirit of wisdom and understanding, the spirit of counsel and might, the spirit of knowledge and the fear of the Lord. I also loose the Holy Spirit of Jesus into these places."

> For curses, I release blessings
> For jealousy, I release compersion.*
> For envy, I release comfort and contentment.
> For malice and spite, I release goodwill.
> For slander, I release compliment and praise.
> For hatefulness, I release love.
> For meanness, I release goodness.
> For deceitfulness and lying, I release truth.
> For conniving and scheming, I release openness and honesty.
> For treachery and backstabbing, I release faithfulness.
> For theft, I release, giving.
> For murder and death, I release life.
> For trickery, I release honesty.
> For greed, I release generosity.
> For torment, I release contentment.

For destroying and destruction, I release building and edification.

Compersion is wholehearted participation in the happiness of others. It is the sympathetic joy we feel for somebody else, even when their positive experience does not involve or benefit us directly.

Defeating Words with Words

Father in Heaven, I reply to the vicious, poisonous words that have been spoken against me and mine this day. I refute those words and I break the power of those words in the name of your precious Son, Jesus Christ.

I cover the speakers of those words with love and forgiveness and with the blood of Christ. I thank you for saving their souls and I bless them in your Holy Name.

May they realize the error of speaking negatively and repent and be forgiven for these trespasses. In the name of Jesus Christ. Amen.

Order my Steps, Govern my Life

Lord, I give you permission and invite you to intervene in my life to order my steps and govern my life. May all my steps, even the smallest, be ordered by you and not me. I submit my will to you and give you permission to govern my life.

If I meet someone new, if it be a person that I should know, then I thank you for the divine appointment. However, if this person is someone that I should not know, I give you permission to use whatever avenue that you choose to warn me to stay away. Thank you, Lord. In Jesus' name, Amen.

Note: The words; "If this be a person that I should know"

"If this be a person that I should not know."
will solicit movement on the part of the Holy Spirit
rather quickly. When I use these words, I can know in real-time the
answer from the Lord. *This knowledge is worth
more than pure silver or fine gold. Start using it!*

Assign your Holy Warring Angels

Holy warring angels, whether in my absence or presence, I assign you to stand shoulder to shoulder around my home, my car, and all my interests, property, and possessions, so that no harm may penetrate.

Holy warring angels, I assign you to stand shoulder to shoulder around all my descendants and loved ones and their families. Their homes, cars, and all their interests, property, and possessions so that no harm may penetrate.

Prophetic dream of September 18th, 2013

"The Sheets"

I was an observer at a church service, there were housing units at one end of this grassy field and a fairly large church at the other end. After the service, everyone went outside onto the field, where we all noticed something strange. Different colored sheets were descending from way up beyond the clouds all in a row across the lawn from the church to the houses. The sheets were just out of reach even for the tallest person. Some tried to climb up on something to try to grab ahold of the sheets but when they did the sheets behaved like a rainbow to them and would simply disappear.

I watched as they tried different ways to touch the sheets. I heard someone exclaim "these sheets are descending from heaven to Earth, we can pull the kingdom of our Lord down to earth". I saw a woman come out of her house right where the sheets began, with a bunch of different colored sheets and she kept throwing them up to try to make contact with the descending sheets. She did intersect with them but could not pull them down.

When suddenly, she had the idea to use the same color sheet and that may be the "key." I watched as she took a yellow sheet and walked down until she saw a descending yellow sheet. She tossed her sheet up into the descending sheet and the two sheets fused together. That was the secret, she searched it out and discovered it. Once she had her yellow sheet fused to the holy sheet, she began to pull and tug on it until it did come down to her. All that were there saw what she had done and proceeded to do the same. Their lives would never be the same. End.

This dream tells us that we must always pray the Father's will, as Jesus did. You must set aside your own will in favor of the Father's. The fear of the Lord will lead you to always pray the Father's will. Luke 22:42 At the mount of olives on the very night that Jesus was betrayed by Judas, he prayed; "Father, if thou be willing, remove this cup from me: nevertheless, not my will, but thine, be done."

We are invited to make our prayers, requests, and petitions to the Lord, but we must realize that: **Nevertheless, may his will be done.** If you are unsure of just what the Father's will is… just ask him, he will probably let you know by one of the many avenues that he uses to communicate with you. You may have him answer you before you even get the words out of your mouth. You may hear from him in prophetic dreams and even visions. You may hear from him through his ministers, teachers, and saints, and by what you see and hear during the day. Be ever watchful.

PRAYERS

May God richly bless you and yours. May the blessings of Abraham, whom the Lord blessed in all things be yours.

Matthew 15:11

Not that which goeth into the mouth defileth a man;
But that which cometh out of the mouth, this defileth a man.

The author with his daughter, Christine. His son Wayne and his wife Natalia and their three children Aden, David, and Ryan.

Chapter 10.

THE EVIL USE OF TONGUE AND LIPS

The Lord blessed us with the divine gift of being able to use our words just as he does. It is divine because it is in his image. This is an unfathomable gift, one that comes with immense responsibility and immense potential for abuse and thus for the judgment of Almighty God. Our God takes the perverted use of this gift very seriously and those who dare to use their words for evil will be punished way beyond anything that they could ever have imagined. Nevertheless, His judgments are just and true.

The following is a breakdown of words that are evil and must be avoided. Some of them are quite subtle and you are about to be illuminated in ways that many of you did not know.

Jeremiah 33:3 (call unto me and I will show you great and mighty things that you did not know of.)

Proverbs 21:23 Whoso keepeth his mouth and his tongue, keepeth his soul from troubles.

Matthew 15:11 Not that which goeth into the mouth defileth a man; but that which cometh out of the mouth, this defileth a man.

Matthew 15:18 But those things that proceed out of the mouth come forth from the heart, and they defile a man.

Matthew 12:34 O generation of vipers, how can ye, being evil, speak good things? For out of the abundance of the heart the mouth speaketh.

Luke 6:45 A good man out of the good treasure of his heart bringeth forth that which is good, and an evil man out of the evil treasure of his heart bringeth forth that which is evil: for of the abundance of the heart, his mouth speaketh.

The Liar

The definition of a liar: A person who knowingly utters falsehood; one who declares to another, as a fact, what he knows to be not true, and with an intention to deceive him. A prevaricator (a prevaricator means one who has lied or that lies repeatedly.) a perjurer, a false witness, fabricator, deceiver.

Revelation 21:8 But the fearful, and unbelieving, and the abominable, and murderers, and whoremongers and sorcerers and idolaters and all liars shall have their part in the lake which burneth with fire and brimstone: which is the second death.

Colossians 3:9 Lie not to one another, seeing that ye have put off the old man with his deeds.

Exodus 23:1 Thou shalt not raise a false report: put not thine hand with the wicked.

Proverbs 10:18 He that hidest hatred with lying lips, and he that uttereth a slander, is a fool.

Proverbs 17:4 A wicked doer giveth heed to false lips; and a liar giveth ear to a naughty tongue.

Exodus 23:1 Thou shalt not raise a false report: put not thine hand with the wicked to be an unrighteous witness.

Proverbs 19:5 A false witness shall not be unpunished, and he that speaketh lies shall not escape.

The father of all lies is the Devil. Those who practice lying are exhibiting one of his main characteristics. John 8:44 states: (Ye are of your father, the Devil, and the lusts of your father ye will do. He was a murderer from the beginning, and abode not in the truth, because there is no truth in him. When he speaketh a lie, he speaketh of his own: for he is a liar and the father of it.) These are the words of Jesus.

 I had a prophetic dream years ago in which I saw the Devil, he was walking down the road carrying a satchel in his hand. I had always imagined him as a 12-foot-tall evil angel with incredible power and might. Yet I saw him in this dream as a skinny, old man with a crooked neck. His neck jutted out at the Adam's apple and then went back the other way. Isaiah 14:16 (they that see thee shall narrowly look upon thee, and consider thee, saying is this the man that made the whole earth to tremble, that did shake kingdoms.) I did look upon him that day. Then I saw him put down the satchel and I did look inside of it. This was his "toolbox." I thought; *is that all he has?* I always imagined him as having a whole room full of thousands of tools and devices. Yet I am looking into his satchel and there is only a small quantity of tools.

I then realized that this is all he needs, these same tools have been working well for many centuries. *The first "tool" that I saw was lies*, followed by slander and accusations, I could not see further into the satchel, but I was enlightened that day as to who he really is. Then I remembered Luke 10:19 (behold I give unto you power to tread on serpents and scorpions, and over all the power of the enemy: and nothing shall by any means hurt you.) Also recalled was 1st John 3:8 (he that committeth sin is of the Devil; For the Devil sinneth from the beginning. For this purpose the Son of God was manifested; that He might destroy the works of the Devil.) And 1st John 4:4 (ye are of God, little children, and have overcome them: because greater is he that is in you than he that is in the world.) When Jesus died and was resurrected, he dethroned the Devil. The Devil was no longer the "Prince of this World." But he will remain, although defeated, until the end of the age at which time he will be cast, by Jesus Christ, into the lake of fire. You, as a believer, need to understand your authority in Christ. I have found that I indeed have authority over all the power of the enemy, and I exercise it daily.

I have known many liars, I am sure we all have but I have met only a few that I would consider to be "professional liars," or what is called a prevaricator. These people lie constantly even when the truth would better serve them. They are obsessed with lying and seem to enjoy watching others believe what they have said. It is entertainment to them. They cannot help themselves; they have become so immersed in lying that they simply cannot stop. A lying spirit propels them.

Interestingly enough, I have seen that these professionals do not look the part of a liar. They look like very trustworthy people on the outside, they are exceptionally smooth, and they dress and talk like normal people.

One would never think that almost everything that comes out of their mouths is a lie. They are laughing to themselves, in your face, as they tell lie after lie, and you believe it. In short, they are **extremely believable.** If you encounter a professional liar, I advise you to go "no contact" with that person. Pray for them but excuse yourself from their presence. To be in the mere presence of a prevaricator is a dangerous place to be.

I have found that since I have acquired the fear of the Lord, I can spot them in real-time. The fear of the Lord will keep you.

Wisdom is the primary thing, then understanding, and then knowledge.

Wisdom is the primary thing and out of it proceeds understanding. Understanding means insight into the *real* nature of people and situations. It is much more than smarts. A bright person can be easily fooled, but not so with the one that remains in the fear of the Lord.

The Slanderer

The definition of a slanderer is: A defamer: One who injures another by maliciously reporting something to his prejudice, calumnious; uses slanderous words, speeches, or reports, false and maliciously uttered. One who injures maliciously the reputation of another by uttering false reports to tarnish or impair with false tales, maliciously told, or propagated.

Psalms 101:5 Whoso privily slandereth his neighbour, him will I cut off; Him that hath an high look and a proud heart will not I suffer.

Leviticus 19:16 Thou shalt not go up and down as a talebearer among thy people; neither shalt thou stand against the blood of thy neighbour: I am the Lord.

Proverbs 10:18 He who hideth hatred with lying lips and he that uttereth a slander, is a fool.

The slanderer is kinsmen to the liar. Many times, those two terms are used together (lie and slander) The liar invents lies and slanders with them, but the slanderer hears lies and runs with them. The slanderer engages in spreading it around or "publishing" it. Psalm 101:5 tells us that the slanderer will be cut off.

Years ago, I saw first-hand how a liar and his slanderers work. There was a woman that this liar wanted to get rid of, so he made up a bunch of lies about her and then solicited some people to help him spread these incredible lies against her as far and wide as he could. These slanderous people were only too happy to help him do this. **They were eager to help**, this was something that they very much enjoyed. Even though they all knew that none of this was true!

The poor woman was not even aware that there was a massive slander campaign against her. This was all done behind her back, and she never would have thought that this person (the liar) would be capable of doing something like that. He went about his dirty business like a snake, hidden in the grass, undetectable until it was too late. In the darkness he did operate, the Devil's kingdom is a kingdom of darkness, and his servants operate in that darkness.

I noticed that these people would accidentally, "on purpose" just happen to "bump into" the people that they wanted to spread these lies to, engage in normal conversation, and then "drop" the bomb on them regarding this poor woman. They did this every day going from one person to another sometimes in public or at their businesses and sometimes even at their homes. They were all highly skilled at this evil and conducted this campaign in person, even going so far as to make a personal visit to the police department.

They followed this up with a telephone attack, they would spend a good part of the day and evening calling everyone that they knew that would be interested in hearing about this woman, and after talking for a bit they would quite skillfully, and at the precise moment, drop the bomb.

The telephone attack was followed up by a social media attack. This was the last platform that they used because this one could be detected by her or those that favored her. It was only when they did not care about being discovered anymore that they removed their "smiling masks," that is when they kicked off the social media campaign.

Remember, one of the definitions of a slanderer is: One who injures maliciously the reputation of another by uttering false reports to tarnish or impair *with false tales*, maliciously told, or propagated.

The sad part is they were successful in this evil operation and that the woman who was the target of their lies and slander believed that this liar was her *best friend!*

The victim of these lies and slander was fooled by these servants of Satan. Remember, your adversary seeks to fool you and trick you. She lacked discernment and had to rely on her abilities to protect herself. If she would have had the Holy Spirit and the fear of the Lord, she could have avoided this catastrophe. Delete the liar and the slanderer from your life but pray that they be convicted of their sins and repent. You must forgive them and ask the Lord to forgive them also.

Two Prophetic Dreams about Lies and Slander

Dream Number One

I dreamed that I was asking the Lord for something very prayerfully. I was tired of doing nothing. Three days later it seemed as if the Lord was answering my prayer.

I took someone to a college in Austin, Texas. I was sitting in the back of a class and began to paint on a blank canvas. I was showing a student what I was doing when the professor walked in from the back and started to admire the art. He began to suggest adding things which I did. It was the beginning of a very mutually beneficial relationship. When we were through, with his help, it was truly an amazing work.

After class, we began to talk, and he took me to another room and showed me what they were working on. I was impressed but he lacked a few things that I began to show him. He was very grateful and asked if I could come back and help him finish this project. I said yes and I came in every day for about a week. I set him up very well. My knowledge and experience were just what he needed. Together we finished his project. I was not looking to get anything out of it, I was just happy to help. He was a genuine person, a good man. I was so happy to know him.

The next day I was leaving but I promised to help him with any future projects that he might have. About that time his contact at the college, a red-haired lady came up to him and said that she had some very bad news. She began to slander me as someone who was out to get the facility's money and that I was really bad news. She told him he had better get rid of me right away. She told him that I was on the phone with my girlfriend all morning long conspiring against him and the college and that we had a malevolent plan against them. I did not know why she told him all of that right in front of me until I realized that she could not even see me standing there. The Lord let me see what she was up to. I looked at him and saw that he was believing all her lies. After all, he knew her for years and me for days. He needed her to keep him in the college, but if he would have thought about it, he would have realized that I could not have possibly been on the phone with my girlfriend all morning because I was with him!

I was going to point that out to him as a baseless lie for starters and then go on from there to expose all her lies until I realized that it was no use. He would never believe me anyway. **It was much more comfortable for him to believe the lies;** the Devil had once again overpowered truth with lies. I remember thinking "I thought there was power in truth." I also remembered an attorney telling me in real life, years ago, "Wendell, if you think you can go into that courtroom and tell the truth and the Lord will be with you, you are much more naïve than we thought." We live in a fallen world.

Dream Number Two

In this dream, I was working for a company and doing very well and was happy. I did them a lot of good and they did me the same. I was in a truck with a younger man, and we were going into the company's storage area to pick up some things.

As we drove up to the entrance we saw "Jim" across the street. I thought "oh no" I hope he does not see us but just then he looked over and noticed us. I remember thinking he is wearing his brown and white shirt and I know he feels very powerful and arrogant when he wears that shirt. He was also prone to causing trouble when given the opportunity.

I said let's just hurry up and get in here and out because Jim has already seen us and could be up to no good. So, we went in the entrance and down an alleyway, and there in front of us was an obstacle, some debris in our path. It slowed us down because I had to get out of the truck and clear it away.

I told the man that I was with "Ok, that's two, one is that Jim saw us and two is that we were bogged down with this obstruction. We kept on, when we got to the storage unit the key would not go into the lock and we struggled with that for a long time until we finally got it in. I said, "Ok, that's three." We loaded up what we came for and started out the other side of the alleyway when *here they come!* Three security guys in a jeep to confront us. We showed them our badges and keys and told them we have authority to be here and that we and they both worked for the same company. They told us that they received a call about two "inebriated" employees that were scrounging around the storage facility and had no business being there. I told them "Do we look inebriated?" to which they replied, "Well, some people can hold their liquor quite well." I saw that they were determined to "get us." They wanted to get us, it fit their purposes to get us. To do so worked for them, it made them look good to the boss, after all, it showed that they received a call, responded immediately, and apprehended two scoundrels, good for you!

When they made a report to the boss, he was surprised that the scoundrels were the two of us, (of all people.) He said, "You just don't know about people sometimes, and it's good you found out about those two now, instead of later." He congratulated his security team on "weeding us out." In reality, he just weeded out his two best and most loyal employees based on a pack of lies and slander. We live in a fallen world.

The Curser

The definition of a curser is: One who utters a wish of evil against another; to imprecate evil upon. (imprecate means to call for mischief or injury to fall upon.) To execrate. (execrate means to declare to be evil,) To subject to evil; to vex, harass or torment with great calamities. Malediction: (malediction means: A magical word or phrase uttered with the intention of bringing about evil or destruction; a curse.) the expression of a wish of evil upon another. To bring affliction; torment; great vexation.

Proverbs 26:2 As the bird by wandering, as the swallow by flying, so the curse causeless shall not come.

Deuteronomy 30:7 And the Lord, thy God will put all these curses upon thine enemies and on them that hate thee, which persecuted thee.

Deuteronomy 28:15 But it shall come to pass, if thou wilt not hearken unto the voice of the Lord thy God, to observe to do all his commandments and his statutes which I command thee this day; that all these curses shall come upon thee and overtake thee.

Deuteronomy 28:45 Moreover all these curses shall come upon thee, and shall pursue thee, and overtake thee, till thou be destroyed; because thou hearkenedst not unto the voice of the Lord thy God, to keep his commandments and his statutes which he commanded thee.

Being cursed is much more common than you may think. There are many servants of Satan that you would *never suspect*, that are engaging in this practice. Some of them could even be in your own church, or at your place of employment. They could be your neighbors, friends, and acquaintances. They may even be in your own families.

    Know this; that not all these "cursers" are into witchcraft, many of them are just people who are mean, jealous, and hateful, of you, they are spiteful, bitter, envious, and resentful. Jealous of your happiness, jealous of your success. They bitterly resent you and are secretly envious of you, even though they are smiling in your face and even flattering you. You can pick up on who they are by noticing spitefulness, which is usually out in the open, remember, also those who tend to mimic you and do what you do are a sign to you, remember imitation is the sincerest form of flattery. Please do not disregard it, even if it is coming from someone close to you. The Holy Spirit will reveal these people to you, but you must *ask him*, and you must be willing to accept his advice no matter how difficult it may seem at the time. It sometimes takes courage because the truth can be very painful. The fear of the Lord will give you insight into the true nature of the people and situations that you must face. You must walk through life with *the Holy Spirit* and with *the fear of the Lord*, in order to lead a life free from the negative effects brought about by the curser.

The impenetrable, shed, and resurrected blood of Christ is the coating that you must wear so that any curses will have to slip right off. Just like rain slips off a raincoat.

The prayers that I use to stay protected from curses are given to you in chapter 9. The whole armor of God. The impenetrable hedge of protection. Covering your loved ones and descendants. Breaking off curses. I say those four prayers almost daily, that is how important it is, trust me.

Please notice that these "curses" that we are referring to here, are only the curses that proceed out of the mouths of the servants of Satan.

Those that curse you out of jealousy, or for other reasons, and are not into witchcraft, are not the servants of Satan.

There are five sources of curses to you that you must understand.

1. The curses that proceed out of the mouth of God
2. The curses that you have unwittingly pronounced upon yourself
3. The curses that have been "cast" at you by the servants of Satan
4. The curses that came from those who are or were in authority over you.
5. The curses that came down through your bloodline in the form of generational curses.

All of these are explained thoroughly in my book "A Call to Prayer." I highly recommend that you obtain a copy if you do not already have one. Once again, in this word study of "The Curser," we are only dealing with the curses that have been cast at you by the servants of Satan.

The curses that came down through your bloodline, in the form of generational curses, are explained in detail in my book "Holy Blood Transfusion." This book is a "must-have" it will show you how to once and for all break these curses off from not only yourself but your descendants as well.

The curse "causeless" shall not come. (Proverbs 26:2) These curses can and will be originated and "cooked up" to be cast at you and yours, but without a cause, they will go back to the sender, seven-fold. In these last days, you should be able to live your lives totally protected from the curses of them that hate you, and they are out there, my friends, believe me.

I have seen people in other countries that were cursed into oblivion by witchcraft. I remember this young man; he came from a good family they were well off and lived in a nice house. He was a very promising baseball player. He was highly skilled and very athletic and quick. Everyone just knew he was destined to play in the major leagues. He beheld a very promising life ahead of him, but he had a girlfriend that was a witch. I'm sure he didn't think that much about it at the time, but it came to pass that he found some other woman and jilted the witch. She reacted with intense rage, her love for him turned to hate in an instant. He was alone, both his parents had passed away. She was not alone; she had the power of her "coven" of witches. They cursed that poor young man into absolute insanity. He couldn't even talk anymore. He could not take care of himself or feed himself. The neighbor ladies would cook food for him and just leave it on his porch. One night I heard the sound of glass breaking for hours. (I was staying in the house next door to his.) The next morning, we all got up and saw that he had taken a baseball bat and smashed every window in the house. He was tormented and afflicted. I saw all of this with my own eyes. We would see him walking around the town and sometimes hand him money. He would immediately go to a market and get some candy and snacks. Such a tragedy all brought on by the servants of Satan and curses. Curses are very real my brothers and sisters.

The curser is one of the most dangerous subjects in this word study. If someone is cursing you from afar and in the darkness, how would you even know about it? If you do find out, how on earth will you fight it off? Well, now you know and have the weapons to defeat it. 1st John 4:4 You are of God, little children, and have overcame *them* for greater is he that is in you than he that is in the world. Luke 10:19 Behold, I give unto you power to tread on serpents and scorpions, and over all the power of the enemy, and nothing shall by any means hurt you. Stand on those verses, and others, and pray the four prayers that are in chapter nine, and you will overcome. Revelation 12:11 For I overcame him by the blood of the Lamb, and the word of *my* testimony.

I found out, through the revelation of the Holy Spirit just who was cursing me, and there were more than a few. When I was a young man, I did not believe in witchcraft or curses, I thought it to be non-sense. That is until I began to see that something was terribly wrong, others in my life saw it also. I had to acknowledge the truth about it and the Lord gave me the knowledge of how to defeat it. I only wish I had known this back then because I suffered much. That is one of the reasons that I have authored this book. To give you a heads up about the "curser," he exists, and he is out to cause you much damage, hurt, pain, and suffering. If you have no protection, you will indeed incur this and much more.

Now I am protected from the curser and his curses. I am a child of God, and he has delivered to me the knowledge and prayers to defeat the enemy. One of the big mistakes that I made in my life was to believe that I was protected from all of this simply because I believed that Jesus Christ is the Son of God and that I went to church and refrained from sin, well, most of it anyway. I found out the hard way that this is "not enough." If you think that you are truly a Son or Daughter of the most-high God, then I say to you check yourself; do you follow ALL his commandments? Do you recognize and listen to his voice? Jesus said, "As many that follow my commandments and hear my voice."

John 10:27 My sheep hear my voice, and I know them, and they follow me.

I had to make a *much deeper commitment* to the Lord and really keep ALL his commandments and listen for his voice and follow Him **before he revealed to me how to defeat witchcraft and the curser.** I have left a prayer for you in chapter 9, this is the one the Holy Spirit gave to me to defeat the curser. It is under the sub-heading (Breaking off curses.)

The Betrayer

The definition of a betrayer is: One who betrays, a traitor. To deliver into the hands of an enemy by treachery or fraud, in violation of trust. To violate by fraud or unfaithfulness; as, to betray a trust.

Matthew 26:14-16 Then one of the twelve, called Judas Iscariot, went unto the chief priests, and said unto them, What will ye give me, and I will deliver him unto you? and they covenanted with him for thirty pieces of silver and from that time he sought opportunity to betray him.

Luke 22:22 And truly the Son of man goeth, as it is determined; but woe unto that man by whom he is betrayed.

Matthew 24:10 And then shall many be offended, and shall betray one another, and shall hate one another.

Psalms 41:9 Yea, mine own familiar friend, in whom I trusted, which did eat of my bread hath lifted up his heel against me.

Luke 6:45 A good man out of the good treasure of his heart bringeth forth that which is good; and an evil man out of the evil treasure of his heart bringeth forth that which is evil: for of the abundance of the heart his mouth speaketh.

Proverbs 4:24 Put away from thee a froward mouth, and perverse lips put far from thee.

Luke 22:48 But Jesus said unto him, Judas, betrayest thou the Son of man with a kiss?

Isaiah 33:1 Woe to thee that spoilest, and thou wast not spoiled; and dealest treacherously, and they dealt not treacherously with thee! When thou shalt cease to spoil, thou shalt be spoiled; and when thou shalt make an end to deal treacherously, they shall deal treacherously with thee.

Betrayal is a vast subject. There is much information in the Bible on this. Some people have suffered much more betrayal than others, some of the reasons are inherited generational curses and it also seems like those who inhabit the office of the prophet attract betrayers. Even though you are a child of God, you are still subject to betrayal because the enemy will never stop what he is doing, he will ramp it up as the end of the age nears. If you are a threat to the kingdom of darkness, you are a prime candidate for betrayal. Please do not think that you are automatically protected from it. When you let your guard down, the enemy will strike.

    You cannot have betrayal without trust. Trust is earned, not given. Many times, I have seen in my own life and the lives of many others that I have known a kind of trust that is *given*, and that is called "unmerited trust." This kind of trust is extremely dangerous to you. You are walking on thin ice anytime you "give" unmerited trust. This will rarely work out for you, and it very well could destroy you, and yours. Please refrain from giving unmerited trust to anybody. Do it for yourself first and then for your children and grandchildren. Ask the Lord to show you any "betrayers" in your life. Ask Him to reveal and expose them to you first and then to everyone else. Look for prophetic dreams that are called "warning dreams" these dreams will shine a light on just who is planning to betray you. That is how I have overcome the betrayers in my life. The Lord is faithful to warn his saints, but you must be listening and watching for it. You also must be willing to accept it once you hear it because the truth can many times be rather difficult to embrace. It may go against everything that you are currently thinking. Ask the Lord for the courage to accept the truth and to act on it accordingly.

The fear of the Lord will expose betrayers for you. If you have the fear of the Lord, you will not have to fear anything else. You will not have to worry about betrayers and fear everything that comes along. If you do not have the fear of the Lord, ask the Holy Spirit to lead you into it. Seek it for it will save your life.

The Opposer

The definition of an opposer is: One that opposes, one who acts in opposition; one who resists; to set against with a view of counterbalance or countervail. (countervail means to act against with equal force or power. and thus, to hinder, defeat, destroy or prevent effect.)

The opposer seems to oppose everything that you try to do. Have you experienced that?

Many years ago, in my life, there was a man who worked for me and seemed to oppose me at every turn, even in minor, seemingly innocuous, trivial things. I noticed it, after a season, and I asked myself why he would want to oppose everything that I do and say. He seemed to have a better way or an opposing view. He seemed to work very hard at persuading me to not carry through on my own intentions, to shut me down. He would say things like "well, you don't want to do that, Wendell." Or "that will never fly." "Are you sure about that?" "Why don't you do this instead." Oftentimes, casting doubt on my abilities and decisions.

The opposer is a sower of doubt, self-doubt, being sowed into you on a regular basis, officiously, that is to say, the opposer acts as an "official voice," having much authority, (an *undue* influencer,) the key words here are "acts" and "undue." So, one day I decided to set a trap for him. I came up with something that I used as bait for the opposer to see if he took it and would run with it. I told him about my new idea, (which was something that I just cooked up for the purpose of confirmation.) Sure enough, he grabbed onto that with much force and tried his best to *block me* from implementing it. I watched and observed with much intensity as he produced argument after argument of why this was such a bad idea and would never work. He just exposed himself, he was revealed to me that day. I discovered him. Needless to say, this individual was banished from my life from that day on.

Once I got rid of the "opposer" things began to function normally for me. I no longer had this "negative voice" in my ear, and I felt as if a very heavy weight had been lifted off me. I am all for taking advice, and I listen to everyone that offers it, but if I discern that someone is an opposer, I cut them off rapidly.

On a side note, let me introduce you to "the blocker." This person is kin to the opposer. They will try to block you in any way they can from being able to do what you need to do, find what you need to find, see what you need to see, hear what you need to hear, obtain what you need to obtain, and meet who you need to meet. Many opposers are blockers but not all of them. Blockers will try to cover you up; they don't want anyone to notice you. In their minds, you are "not allowed" to talk to certain people or do certain things. Who put them in charge of you? I have had blockers go to great lengths to try to block me from talking to certain people, as in a meeting or a church service. You are not allowed to talk to anyone who might be helpful to you. Several times in my life I have had blockers "sidestep" right between myself and someone I was having a conversation with, leaving me staring at the back of the blocker's head. Can you even imagine that? Cut off in mid-sentence. How desperate is that? I have also had them try to cut off my conversation with someone by coming up behind the person that I am speaking with and with a very loud voice, call out to them so that the person I am talking to turns around and now, suddenly, they are not talking with me anymore they are speaking with the blocker instead.

How do you identify an opposer, blocker, or for that matter any of the subjects in this word study? You first acquire the fear of the Lord. That is the beginning of wisdom. Please read and reread chapter 7, titled "The Fear of the Lord".

The Gossip

The definition of a gossip is: One who reveals secrets, one who goes about as a talebearer or scandalmonger. A gossiper is a person who has privileged information about people and proceeds to reveal information to those who have no business knowing it.

Psalms 34:13 Keep thy tongue from evil, and thy lips from speaking guile.

Proverbs 20:3 It is an honour for a man to cease from strife; but every fool will be meddling.

Psalms 41:5-7 Mine enemies speak evil of me, he speaketh vanity; his heart gathereth iniquity to itself; when he goeth abroad he telleth it.

Proverbs 6:16-19 These six things doth the Lord hate; yea, seven are an abomination to him: A proud look, a lying tongue, and hands that shed innocent blood, a heart that deviseth wicked imaginations, feet that be swift in running to mischief, a false witness that speaketh lies, and he that soweth discord among brethren.

The gossip is the "gateway" to most of the rest of the more deadly word usages. It seems almost innocent, and everybody engages in it. Little do they know that this is a path to the more cynical and dangerous uses of words that the talebearer, tattler, and busybody engage in. Your enemy, the Devil does not throw everything at you at once. He works progressively and incrementally to destroy you. He is cunning and patient. You are introduced to gossip first because that seems to be relatively harmless, however little by little you will slowly slip into worse, and worse. Your enemy, the Devil operates in a very subtle and slow, almost indiscernible manner. Please recognize that gossip is not pleasing to our Lord, and it is dangerous to you and yours. If left unchecked you will slide down a slippery slope, ever so slowly.

I remember as a child of about ten years old, I was introduced to gossip by an older woman who engaged in it frequently. I just did not know too much about it at that time, since I was just a kid. She would come over to my grandparents' home and start gossiping about others that I knew. I saw right away that she enjoyed it. She was eager to gossip. At first, I was interested in hearing about all of that, it sounded so enticing, but as she went along, I became bored and did not want to dwell on it. I did, however, find some of this gossip quite juicy. As they say, "juicy tidbits." Well, the woman moved out of the area, and I had no contact with gossipers after that. I grew up and eventually I encountered more gossipers.

I remember going out to eat with my wife and one or two other couples on many occasions. After initial conversations, I noticed that the conversation would eventually drift to gossip. I still did not know that it was wrong. I did not at that time know what the Bible said about gossiping.

As I got older and into the Word of God, I did see that it was speech that was not right in his eyes. When conversations with others would turn to gossip, I would politely tell them that we had crossed a red line and now we're slipping into gossip. That usually stopped the gossiping.

Please do not engage in gossip, realize that it is a gateway into more dangerous word usage. There is certainly nothing innocent about it. If you have been guilty of gossip you need to repent for it and ask that your words be washed away in the blood of His precious Son, Jesus Christ never to be remembered against you again and so that you will not have to give an account for it at your final judgment because it does not even exist anymore. Please do not let unrepented gossip befall you.

The Whisperer

The definition of a whisperer is: One who whispers. A tattler: one who tells secrets; a conveyer of intelligence secretly. A backbiter. One who slanders secretly in a low voice.

Proverbs 16:28 A froward man soweth strife; and a whisperer separateth chief friends.

Froward means perverse, deceitful, and false.

Ecclesiastes 21:28 A whisperer defileth his own soul and is hated wheresoever he dwelleth.

Ecclesiastes 28:13 Curse the whisperer and double tongued; for such have destroyed many that were at peace.

Ecclesiastes 5:14 Be not called a whisperer and lie in wait with thy tongue: For a foul shame is upon a thief and an evil condemnation upon the double tongue.

Romans 1:29 Being filled with all unrighteousness, fornication, wickedness, covetousness, maliciousness, full of envy, murder, debate, deceit, malignity, whispers.

Simple whisperings can truly separate good friends. I have seen many instances of this over the years. Whisperers are the ones who drop hints, insinuations, and innuendos so quietly and seemingly so innocently just during normal conversations, that the hearer of these words would never expect that they were crafted and very carefully dropped at the precise time and place to cause the hearer to begin to reflect and think long, as well as to think wrong. If you suspect you are thinking in this manner, you should go back and reflect on the person that got you to think like this. This did not just come out of your own head. It had a source, and that source was most likely a whisperer. Sometimes a trusted person in your life and other times just someone looking to cause trouble, sadly just for the entertainment that they derive from this mischief.

    The person hearing the whisperer would never believe that they were the target of an insidious planned attempt to start the ball rolling on malevolent intentions. They are the planters of negative seeds in your head and many times they are people who you truly believe are your friends or at least people that you thought would never do something like that. These seeds take time to grow, the whisperer knows this and is very patient. They are playing the long game. They also are extremely confident of not being discovered. The Holy Spirit can bring this to your attention through warning dreams and the many other avenues of his choice. The fear of the Lord will keep you from falling victim to the whisperer. You, having the fear of the Lord will see right through them and they will be exposed in your eyes, in real-time. You will not have to go home and pray about it, contemplate it, and meditate on it. You will immediately know it *when you hear it*. That, my friend, is a good place to be.

The Backbiter

The definition of a backbiter is: One who censors, slanders, reproaches, or speaks evil of the absent. Secret calumny, secret slander. (calumny means defamation of character.)

Proverbs 25:23 The north wind driveth away rain; so doth an angry countenance a backbiting tongue.

Proverbs 15:1-3 Lord, who shall abide in thy tabernacle? Who shall dwell in thy holy hill? He that walketh uprightly, and worketh righteousness, and speaketh the truth in his heart. He that backbites not with his tongue, nor doeth evil to his neighbor, nor taketh a reproach up against his neighbor.

2nd Corinthians 12:20 For I fear that when I come, I shall not find ye as I would and that I shall be found unto you such as ye would not: Lest there be debates, envying's, wraths, strifes, backbiting, whisperings, swellings, tumults.

We have all probably experienced a backbiting person in our lives. Many times, this backbiter seems like one of your best friends and you would never believe that they are trying their best to harm you and sabotage you in any way they can, all while remaining elusive and undetected, even flattering you and smiling in your face.

If you have any suspicions that someone is secretly backbiting, it may be the Holy Spirit trying to warn you. Ask Him to show you, he may do this in a prophetic dream, or through the words of others. Pay heed to any warnings from other people. Pay heed to the warnings of the Holy Spirit that you may be experiencing in your dreams. As foreign and unrealistic as it may seem to you, it may indeed be the truth. Ask Him to reveal any backbiters in your life and he probably will, but you must have the courage to accept it and act upon it. The truth is sometimes very hard to wrap your head around, but nevertheless, you must accept the truth no matter how much it may hurt at the time. In the end, you will have saved you and yours a multitude of damage, hurt, pain, and suffering.

Always remember, the backbiter works in secret, he speaks evil of the absent. Secret slander and defamation of your character is his game. An undermining spirit animates him. This spirit works to sabotage and undermine you in an incremental way. Beware of the backbiter. You cannot stand in the same arena as the backbiter, you will lose. You can only defeat him through prayer. This is a spiritual creation, and it must be broken in the spirit. You as carnal man cannot defeat him on your own. Ask the Lord to shine his Holy Glory Light on the backbiter to reveal and expose them to everybody. You cannot possibly expect to expose the backbiter on your own.

The backbiter himself is a victim of the powers in the second heaven. the evil, wicked, and demonic spirits that Paul spoke of in Ephesians 6:12. Put on the whole armor of God to protect yourself from this damaging entity. Remember that the backbiter is a human being, and you must pray for them to be delivered from that evil spirit. That is how you win, on your knees before the Lord.

The Accuser

The accuser is one of the most dangerous of all the subjects in this word study. He is actually doing the work of the Devil. One of the titles that describe the Devil is "The Accuser." The Bible says that he accuses the brethren day and night before the Lord. Have you ever met an accusing person? I am sure that you have. Have you ever been accused of something so outrageous that you wonder how could they ever have come up with that? I have been accused of many things that I could not have done even on my worst day.

I recall, when I was only about 20 years old, I was staying at a place not far from my grandparents' new home in California. They had a nice little garden there and were growing carrots and potatoes along with tomatoes and other vegetables.

One Sunday afternoon, some other relatives dropped by while I was there. I began showing them the garden and around the house. This was their first time visiting this new location. Then in the afternoon, I went back to my place. The other relatives left later that afternoon. That evening and as soon as they got home, they called the Los Angeles County Sheriff's Office and accused me of planting marijuana in my grandparent's garden.

The deputies rushed straight over to that location, kicked the door in and drug my grandparents out of the house (they being in their mid-seventies), and had them face down in the backyard while they rummaged through the garden to find the contraband plants. They kept asking where I was, but my grandparents did not know. They also ransacked their house, based on the erroneous information that was given to them *by my loved one*. They were stumped by the plants because they were small and just coming up. and had to call in the Los Angeles police department, narcotics bureau. It took several hours for them to drive all the way from Los Angeles to the location. When they arrived, they confirmed that all those plants were just vegetables. The accuser strikes! The only thing that was accomplished was that my grandparents spent about three hours handcuffed on their stomachs in the backyard of their new home.

What on earth would possess someone to make a false allegation of such magnitude? If I would have been there, I know they would have called me a scum bag and beat me up, maybe even shot me. All for nothing, well, I did not know how to process all that had transpired. I was shocked. It was not until years later that I realized just why these people made such a horrendous accusation. They were animated and inspired by the demonic forces in the second heaven that Paul talks about in Ephesians 6:12. I realized that I could not even blame them for what happened. They were just as much a victim as was I and my grandparents.

Now that I am much older, I can attest to the fact that these same people that called the police on me, that day, have made a lifetime of accusations against me and mine. (that is what I call "toxic people.") All were false allegations. The allegations have always been followed up and found to be without merit. But that is ok. No one is ever going to make them pay for their false allegations and lies. Only God, Himself that is. You must deal with them through prayer, asking the Lord to convict them of this activity, and lead them into repentance. You must forgive them and ask the Lord to forgive them as well.

You cannot stand in the arena with an accuser, you will eventually lose big time. They keep slinging allegations at you one after another hoping that one of them will stick. Many allegations that are leveled against you, will be unknown to you. They secretly fire off flaming arrows at you that you will not ever even know about, all while smiling in your face! If you have an accuser in your life you need to go "no contact" with them. That will greatly reduce the amount and severity of their attacks, but it will not stop them altogether because the nature of Satan is one of relentlessness. He is never going to stop what he is doing, in fact, he is going to ramp it up, especially in these times when we are under severe attack. The only way to defeat the accuser is in prayer. You can put a stop to them. I ask the Lord to make me invisible to the accuser. To get my name out of their heads and get their attention off me. I rebuke and bind the demonic and cast them into the pit in the name of Jesus Christ, and seal them in there with his blood. This is an ongoing battle; it is not just a "one and you're done" kind of thing. That is why it is called spiritual warfare because that is exactly what it is, the good news is that you can neutralize the accusers in your life and be free of their dangerous activities. Pray for them to be led by God and not the Devil. Ask the Lord to grant them repentance. Forgive them and ask the Lord to forgive them also.

The Talebearer

The definition of a talebearer is: A person who maliciously gossips or reveals secrets. A blabber, and newsmonger. A person who officiously tells tales; one who impertantly communicates intelligence or anecdotes and makes mischief in society by his officiousness.

Proverbs 11:13 A talebearer revealeth secrets; but he that is of faithful spirit concealeth the matter.

Proverbs 26:22 The words of a talebearer are as wounds, and they go down into the innermost parts of the belly.

Proverbs 20:19 He that goeth about as a talebearer revealeth secrets; therefore, **meddle not with him that flattereth with his lips.**

Proverbs 26:20 Where there no wood is, the fire goeth out; so, where there is no talebearer, the strife ceaseth.

Leviticus 19:16 Thou shalt not go up and down as a talebearer among thy people; neither shall thou stand against the blood of thy neighbor: I am the Lord.

Have you met the talebearer? They differ from some of the other subjects in our word study that are similar such as the gossip, backbiter, and tattler in that the talebearer tells tales with the goal of causing "mischief" in your life. They tell these tales with great malice in mind. They kindle a fire against you and keep feeding it so that it never goes out. They "tend" the fire which they themselves started in your life, sometimes for years, going undetected, smiling, and offering "flattery" to you and even praising you all the while. All this while having your worst interests in mind. Having a spiritual "knife in your back." They are confident of not being discovered or exposed.

    They are revealing secrets and publishing them around for all to hear. Not only revealing secrets but fabricating lies and mixing them with some truth to make them much harder to discern. Twisting your words, embellishment, and exaggeration are three of their "tools." They are dragging you down progressively and incrementally. Little by little. The talebearer, undiscovered will ultimately destroy you and yours, like a fire, they will "consume." These people are extremely clever, they think of themselves as "way ahead" of you. They operate with much confidence and arrogance thinking that you will never discover them. You probably would never have discovered them, you would have lived your entire life being oblivious to their existence, *but for God*.

This book has been designed to give you a "heads up" as to all of the subjects in this chapter and do not forget that if you see yourself, even slightly see yourself, in any of these subjects, you need to renounce and repent for the words that you have used. Every one of these subjects that we are studying here have to do with words. Words and speech are the subject matter of this entire book. Confess, renounce, recall and repent for any words that *you* have used that may be displeasing unto the Lord. The answer is with the Holy Spirit.

The Tattler

The definition of a tattler is: One who tattles; an idle talker; one that tells tales. A betrayer, fink, informant, rat, snitch, squealer, tattletale.

1st Timothy 5:13 And withal they learn to be idle, wandering about from house to house; and not only idle, but tattlers also and busybodies, speaking things which they ought not.

Proverbs 24:2 For their heart studieth destruction, and their lips talk of mischief.

Psalms 41:5-7 Mine enemies speak evil of me, he speaketh vanity; his heart gathereth iniquity to itself; when he goeth abroad he telleth it.

This tattler is a dangerous person, they will inform others of not only the things that are true about you but also things that are entirely made up. The tattler is famous for telling long tales about others that have no basis in reality, and most of the time the people will believe it. I remember one time in my life I tried to expose a tattler and the people to whom I was talking replied. "Well, why would they say that about him if it wasn't true?" I hit a brick wall on that one. I started to notice that old saying: he who "gets down" first is believed. You will spin your wheels trying to cover the tattler's lies with truth. People have it set in their minds, and *they do not want to change what they have believed.* Some of them even are pleased to believe the tattler if it fits with their own agendas. We live in a fallen world.

Psalms 41:5-7 tells of a person who visits another just for the sole purpose of gathering iniquity or "dirt" on them. They come in speaking vanity as a cover, but their goal is to get as much negative information as they can so that they can twist, embellish, and exaggerate it and spread it far and wide. They are engaging in a massive slander campaign. These people are entertained by their successes. They also have ulterior motives and something to gain by destroying you. Yes, saints, the tattler is dangerous indeed.

Let me mention that the tattler is a natural informant to law enforcement, code enforcement, adult protective services, child protective services or any other authority in your life, such as your supervisor. They will "try to get you in trouble" with your spouse, friends, and family. They will constantly try to put you in "harm's way." They will "squeal" on you for any and everything that they possibly could think of, whether it be *true or not.* You will not see them coming. You would never believe this person was behind all the tattling that you are trying to wade through. You will be wondering where all this is coming from never suspecting the real culprit. The tattler is an expert in getting others to go along with him. He uses a wink and a nod to entice them. Even they will wonder how they could have ever agreed with him, knowing that this is not even true. The tattler's goal is to be able to say "See, everyone is saying that so it must be true." The tattler seeks to involve others to back him up and be his accomplices.

The tattler sounds like a rather benign name, but it is a name that seeks your destruction and even your very soul. When you encounter this person, you need to get away from them as soon as possible. Pray for them to be set free but get away. The Holy Spirit will warn the child of God, it may be through warning dreams, or the many other avenues that he can use to warn you so stay sensitive to the Holy Spirit. The wisdom in the fear of the Lord will keep you from being damaged by the tattler.

The Informer

The definition of an informer is: The one who informs an authority as to bad behavior, this authority could be a parent, a supervisor at work, your landlord, the police, or any other kind of person that is an authority over you in any way. It could be a family member such as a spouse or even a peer. The informer's motive being to harm you and probably to get something in return.

Proverbs 4:24 Put away from thee a froward mouth, and perverse lips put far from thee.

Proverbs 21:23 Whoso keepeth his mouth and his tongue, keepeth his soul from troubles.

Proverbs 17:4 A wicked doer giveth heed to false lips; and a liar giveth ear to a naughty tongue.

Not to confuse an informer with the one who informs to warn. People that warn others are not shown in a negative light but in a positive one. Examples of warnings in the Bible are Mordecai in Esther 2:21-23 In those days, while Mordecai sat in the king's gate, two of the king's chamberlains, Bigthan and Teresh, of those which kept the door, were wroth, and sought to lay hand on the king Ahasuerus. And the thing was known to Mordecai, who told it unto Esther the queen; and Esther certified the king thereof in Mordecai's name. and then inquisition was made of the matter, it was found out; therefore, they were both hanged on a tree; and it was written in the book of chronicles before the king.

Informers of a negative nature in the Bible are Satrap, the Persian. Daniel 6:11-13. Then these men assembled and found Daniel praying and making supplication before his God. They came near, and spake before the king concerning the king's decree; Hast thou not signed a decree, that everyman that shall ask a petition of any God or man within thirty days. Save of thee, O king, shall be cast into the den of lions? Then answered they and said before the king, that Daniel, which is of the children of the captivity of Judah, regardeth not thee, O king, nor the decree that thou hast signed, but maketh his petition three times a day.

This is a textbook example of an informer at work. They are doing the work of the Devil. He is the "accuser," and he does not need your help. Look at the consequences to Daniel; to be thrown into the lion's den. Pretty harsh, and Satrap had no problem giving him over to death. Informers tend to be merciless people. Please do not be guilty of this practice. If you have been the informer before, you need to repent of it. Unless you are informing to warn, such as Mordecai in the book of Esther, you should refrain from this activity and instead pray earnestly for the people that they refrain from the bad behavior that has been brought to your attention. Your words are much better used to tell God how you feel and *pray for the perpetrators* rather than to use your mouth to cause them harm. This is God's way, ask Him to show you, his ways!

The Reporter

The definition of a reporter is: One who reports authorized or unauthorized. A gatherer of information to circulate publicly. To relate from one to another. To give account to be reported.

The reporter is one who feels they must give a report of their day to anyone who will listen. Some of this information is private and should not be divulged. Anytime you tell a story or report on something to others when they repeat it, it may not be entirely as you reported it. I also know that some people who may be on the listening end of your reporting will take in your words, digest them, and twist them around. When they spew them back out, they can be quite toxic, barely resembling what you originally reported.

James 1:26 if any man among you seem to be religious, and bridleth not his tongue, but deceiveth his own heart, this man's religion is in vain.

Mathew 15:18 But those things that proceed out of the mouth come from the heart; and they defile a man.

One example of a "reporter" that I knew, was a woman who went down her list every evening of everyone that she knew and called each of them to give and receive a report. It was a "Job" to her, and she thought that she was just doing her job.

Since we are relational in nature, we are wired to communicate with others, but a reporter takes it to the next level. They proceed without boundaries or restraint, reporting the good and bad of everyone that they know, and receiving likewise. I had this woman report things about me that

I did not want to be public knowledge, what about my privacy? What about the privacy of the other many people that are being reported on each day?

She would sometimes call me to report on others, I noticed that her opening statement on the phone after saying hello was "well, what do you know?" I would think to myself, "well, look at you." I had absolutely no interest in hearing all these stories about people, most of whom I did not even know. I would cut her off right there, saying "I do not want to hear it right now."

She spread stories around that are still circulating years after her death. Many of the people that she reported on have heard these stories and they truly have lost their accuracy over the years. It just depends on who is telling it. Some people "modify" the stories to fit their agendas or how they want others to perceive them. Sad, but true. I can honestly say that in my lifetime I have seen the carnage caused by the reporter and it is not good. They lack the knowledge that I have given you here. They also lack the fear of the Lord. Do not be a "hearer" of reports that come from a reporter, it is beautiful to be able to communicate with others but when the conversation breaks trust and overruns privacy, you now have the wisdom and discernment to notice it and cut it off. If the title of "reporter" fits you, even a little, I pray that in the name of Jesus Christ you be convicted of it and cease.

Reporting is progressive in nature. It will grow upon itself until it becomes second nature and a Goliath to you. Read and study all of these violations of your gift of speech, (as outlined for you in Chapter 10.) Some of them will overlap as you will see. Be advised that although many are born again Christians and follow most if not all of the protocols of Godly speech, it has been my observation that it must never have occurred to them that **these are ALSO a violation of Godly speech.** These people think that they are "home free" and the masters of their tongue when in fact they are deceived. That is why I have included Chapter 10 in this book, with the knowledge that is laid out here, you can truly be the Steward of Speech. Just finish what you started and make sure that none of the subtitles in this chapter resemble you in the least. Ask the Holy Spirit to reveal to you where you are lacking, invite Him to intervene, and give permission to Him. The answer is with the Holy Spirit.

The Detractor

The definition of a detractor is A person who disparages someone or something such as a belittler, fault finder, traducer, disparager, or denigrator.

A diminisher is one who attempts to reduce and lessen you.

To depreciate another, to run them down. (traducer means to speak badly of or tell lies about someone so as to damage their reputation.

Psalms 34:13 Keep thy tongue from evil, and thy lips from speaking guile.

James 4:11 Speak not evil of one another, brethren, he that speaketh evil of his brother, Speaketh evil of the law, and judgeth the law, thou art not a doer of the law but a judge.

Proverbs 4:24 Put away from thee a froward mouth, and perverse lips put far from thee.

I have found the "detractor" at work in my life, many times. You can identify the detractor quite easily. They on the other hand think that they are undetectable for some reason. They just go on month after month, year after year belittling and running down others with seeming impunity. The people they target are the ones that could threaten them and, in many cases, threaten the illusion that they have created of themselves. This false illusion that they have put forth is critical to their plans to move up and forward. These people are truly "diminishers." Their goal is to diminish opinions of you, to reduce you, and to lessen you.

The detractor differs from the other subjects listed in this chapter in that they will belittle and run you down right to your face. Most of the other subjects in this word study do their dirty business behind your back, but not so the detractor. Although most of his work is certainly done behind your back, and in a massive way does he disparage you and publish it to many people. He has no problem disparaging you right to your face and also in the presence of others. One of his goals is to cause you to have a lower opinion of yourself. Remember, as a man thinketh so is he. If he can "bench" you, he will not be found out and you will not move forward. You cannot blame this person because it is not him that is doing this to you. He is animated by the powers in the second heaven. Ephesians 6:12 says: (for we wrestle not against flesh and blood, but against principalities, against powers, against the rulers of the darkness of this world, against spiritual wickedness in high places.) So do not get mad at this person but pray for him, that is how you win. Bind the powers of the second heaven that are manifesting in this person, you can do this under your breath (in your inner man.) even while the detractor is disparaging you *right to your face*, I have done it. First of all, under my breath, I say, "I do not receive that in Jesus' name," then I rebuke and bind the evil, wicked and demonic spirits that are manifesting in this person, by the authority that I have to use the name of Jesus Christ, and I cast all of **you** evil spirits into the pit and seal you in there with the blood of Christ.

I do this at the same exact time that I am looking into the eyes of the detractor and hearing his words in my ears.

These people are many times successful in seducing many others, even most of the congregation in their churches. Most Christians think "Well, I know that this is a man or a woman of God, so why would they say that if it were not true?"

If you think that you can challenge a person that has created a false illusion you are mistaken. This is a battle that you have to fight on your knees. You cannot speak long or fast enough or to enough people to pop their illusion of this person. Ask the Holy Spirit to reveal and expose them. This was created in the spiritual world and must be broken off in the spiritual world. Your carnal man is no match.

The Disseminator

The definition of a disseminator is: One who spreads something widely, a circulator or distributor of information that should be kept private. To publicize and pass on or "put around" this information. (some use social media to accomplish this.)

Proverbs 17:9 He that covereth a transgression seeketh love; but he that repeateth a matter separateth very friends

The disseminator has no regard for those with whom he circulates information about. Even though he knows that this information will hurt you, and even if he does not want to hurt you. He still cannot stop distributing it and spreading it around. The disseminator is obsessed with putting around the information. One reason they do it is for *the recognition of others*, to be noticed and listened to. All the reasons they engage in this behavior are purely selfish. They do get much satisfaction and fulfillment in conducting this task.

It is certainly a task to them; they feel that they are just doing their jobs and all collateral damage is unintended. I have seen parents disseminating information about their children to people that have no business knowing it. They have harmed their own children by not keeping private what should have remained private.

Just look at the other side of this dissemination; the people that are on the "hearing end" of it. What will they do with this confidential information that they have received? Some will simply disregard it, and some will "run" with it and disseminate it even further and still, others will twist, embellish, and exaggerate it and then put it back out there.

Be very careful of whom you let in on your private life. It is best to be wise and of few words. Discern who could be a disseminator and keep them at a distance. Pray for them to be convicted of their sins and to cease these activities. Forgive them for their trespasses. Use the same grace that the Lord uses to forgive you. Keep close to the Holy Spirit and seek the fear of the Lord. *Forgiving them goes a long way toward helping them to end their sin of dissemination.*

The Busybody

The definition of a busybody is: One who is a meddling person. One who officiously concerns themselves with the affairs of others. A gossip, interferer, mischief maker, or eavesdropper. (officiously means assertive in authority in an annoyingly domineering way. Especially regarding petty or trivial matters.)

Thessalonians 3:11 For we hear that there are some which walk among you disorderly, working not at all, but are busybodies.

1st Peter 4:15 But let none of you suffer as a murderer, or as a thief, or as an evildoer, or as a busybody in other men's matters.

Proverbs 20:3 It is an honour for a man to cease from strife, but every fool will be meddling.

You will be able to discern a busybody by noticing the one who meddles and concerns themselves with the affairs of others. These people, in my experience, do not have much of a life themselves but they know *that you do*. They get great satisfaction in getting involved in your business, it becomes a project to them. A long-involved project where they function as your "adviser and handler." Most of the time they are people that are older than you and you deem them wiser just based on their years. They inject themselves into your life and business without invitation. They project *a false illusion* to you of their legitimacy and worth.

I have seen that many of them seem to be under the influence of the imp spirit. That is to say, they function as mischief-makers as they purport to be your back-up and protector. The busybody has destroyed many marriages and friendships. As they act in authority and in a position of "trust" they will drop hints, innuendos, and insinuations on you designed to be "seeds" planted into your head that they water and keep tending until they see fruit. That is "negative fruit." These people are entertained in this manner, they really enjoy their power, and you, all the while thinking that this person is your friend.

If you entertain a busybody, your life will be going backward and not forward, you will be taking one step forward and two steps backward. My friend, you cannot afford to be going backward! Not now, not with everything that is going on. You also cannot afford to lose a spouse or any loyal friends.

You do not want to be feeding a demon with your life!

That is what it amounts to… if you do not expel the busybody.

The Scoffer

The definition of scoffer is: One who scoffs; One that mocks, derides, or reproaches in the language of contempt; a scorner.

The definition of a contemner is: To despise, to consider and treat as mean and despicable; To scorn Psalm 15:2 (to slight, to neglect as unworthy of regard, to reject with disdain. Wherefore do the wicked contemn God.)

2nd Peter 3:3-4 Knowing this first, that there shall come in the last days scoffers, walking after their own lusts, and saying, where is the promise of his coming? For since the fathers fell asleep, all things continue as they were from the beginning of the creation.

Titus 3:2 To speak no evil of no man, to be no brawlers, but gentle showing all meekness unto all.

James 1:26 if any man among you seem to be religious, and bridleth not his tongue, but deceiveth his own heart, this man's religion is in vain.

Proverbs 21:11 When the scorner is punished: the simple are made wise: and when the wise is instructed, he receiveth knowledge.

The scoffer will scoff, jeer, and sneer at others who have a different opinion. They have an uncanny ability to make it seem like they are correct, and all other opinions are ridiculous. The scoffer will heap insolent doubt or derision upon the ideas with which he does not agree. They always must be right, and they are not open to reason. They are dogmatic which is to say; they express personal opinions or beliefs as if they are facts and cannot be doubted. This person *ACTS* as if they are the authority on the matter. The key word is *ACTS*. They will put on an air of officiality and present an illusion to others of their infallibility. They believe they are the final authority on the subject, and that you must not doubt them.

It is sad to say we have many scoffers in the church today. These people are scoffing at the beliefs and practices of other denominations and churches. They have never acquired the fear of the Lord. They have not been able to master their tongue. They feel like they must expose others. They are not simply refuting, or disagreeing with them, they are belittling, disrespecting, and insulting any other person or church that does not agree with them. The scoffer cannot state their opinion without deriding opposing opinions.

Proverbs 21:11 (listed above) shows that the scoffer will be punished, and when he is, the simple will be made wise. I believe the scoffer's punishment will be so great that other scoffers and scorners, seeing it, will cease their activity, out of fear. Galatians 6:7 (be not deceived; God is not mocked: For whatsoever a man soweth, that shall he also reap.) If you are sowing mockery and scoffery, you will undoubtedly reap the same.

The Mocker

The definition of a mocker is: To treat with ridicule or contempt; deride, to mimic as in sport or derision.

The definition of derision is: The act of laughing at in contempt. Contempt manifested by laughter and scorn. Jeremiah 20:3 (I am in derision daily.) An object of derision or contempt, a laughingstock. Lamentations 3, (I was a derision to all my people.)

The definition of a derider is: To laugh at in contempt; to turn to ridicule or make sport of, to mock, to treat with scorn by laughter.

Jude 1:18-19 How that they told you there should be mockers in the last time, who should walk after their own ungodly lusts.

These be they that separate themselves sensual, having not the Spirit.

Isaiah 28:22 Now, therefore, be ye not mockers, lest your bands be made strong: for I have heard from the Lord God of hosts a consumption; even determined upon the whole earth.

The mocking spirit causes some to imitate, sham or fake, cheat, fool dupe or mislead. People who are mockers will mimic others just for fun and deride them. ridiculing them contemptuously. Many times, they also have an impish spirit, they seem to go hand in hand. Please do not be fooled by the impishness of the mocking person. They can seem so child-like, fun-loving, and happy people but the enemy's goal is to kill, steal, and destroy. Yes, that funny, seemingly innocent imp-like behavior is a cover for the Devil as he seeks to cause you damage, hurt, pain and suffering eventually stealing your very soul.

I received a very thorough, direct lesson on the mocker years ago. At that time, I was not aware of the mocker. I hired a young man to work for me in my business and I noticed that he was a very charismatic and likeable person. He had a great sense of humor and seemed to be happy and enjoy life. After about three weeks, I noticed that he would mock some of the older guys that were working there, but not to their faces, He would wait until they went home. Some of the things he said were downright funny. He had us laughing all the time. I never met anyone like that before. His mocking soon turned to outright ridicule. It escalated beyond funny to outright derision and scorn. I noticed that his "humor" had gotten out of hand. He even started mocking some of the other employees right to their faces. He had the uncanny ability to mimic their voices perfectly, even my voice. He could have called my customers or vendors on the phone; mimicked my voice and they would believe they were talking to me. Just imagine the problems that would create. I spoke to him several times asking him to tone it down, some of the others were now starting to complain about him. He had been working there for about six months now, this mocking was introduced to us in a very slow manner. I would liken it to a crock pot, or slow cooker. That is why we never figured it out. It came about little by little until it became unbearable for all of us.

Looking back on it now, I believe that he was so far into it that even though he knew his job was in jeopardy, he could not stop. Finally, I had to fire him. I did not want to because I needed him, and he did a good job. When I let him go, he started yelling "This always happens to me, I go along quite well for a time and then I get fired, that is the story of my life!" So, he left that day, he was upset but not greatly so, he sort of expected it.

He had a friendship with the owner of a nearby business and he went over there to see if they would hire him, and they did.

About two weeks later, that business owner came over to see me and told me that the mocker stole some things, and when he confronted him, he got beaten up. I told him "I never would have thought that he would steal from you, and I did not think he had it in him to beat somebody up." But he certainly did! He was long gone now so at least that was good. About three weeks after that, A police detective called about him. I told them he had been gone about five weeks and I did not have any clue where he would go. They told me that they had a warrant for his arrest. He had so viciously beat someone, in a town about forty miles from us, that the victim was beaten almost to death. He said in all his years he had never seen such a vicious attack on another human being.

We all found it hard to believe that such an innocent, harmless, happy, child-like person could be capable of such violence. That child-like veneer was a cover for the spirit of viciousness. It seemed so out of character for him, yet it was true. A wolf in sheep's clothing I thought. He duped all of us.

Please do not be fooled by the mocker, part of his game is to fool and trick those around him. What you see is not always what you get. Recognize his activities now that you know about them. You should be able to spot a mocking spirit immediately. If I would have had the fear of the Lord at that time, I would not have had to go through what I did with the mocker. The fear of the Lord will keep you from the "snare" of the mocker. If you do not have the fear of the Lord, you need to ask the Holy Spirit to lead you into it.

The Scorner

The definition of a scorner is one who scorns, a contemner, a despiser, a derider.

The definition of a contemner is: To despise, to consider and treat as mean and despicable; to scorn. Psalm 15:2 (to slight, to neglect as unworthy of regard, to reject with disdain. Wherefore do the wicked contemn God.)

The definition of derision is: The act of laughing at in contempt. Contempt manifested by laughter and scorn. Jeremiah 20:3 (I am in derision daily.) An object of derision or contempt, a laughingstock. Lamentations 3, (I was a derision to all my people.)

The definition of a derider is: To laugh at in contempt; to turn to ridicule or make sport of, to mock, to treat with scorn by laughter.

Proverbs 22:10 Cast out the scorner, and contention shall go out; yea, strife and reproach shall cease.

Proverbs 19:29 Judgments are prepared for scorners, and stripes for the back of fools.

Proverbs 13:1 A wise son heareth his father's instruction; but a scorner heareth not rebuke.

Proverbs 21:24 Proud and haughty scorner is his name, who dealeth in proud wrath.

Proverbs 3:34 Surely, he scorneth the scorners; but he giveth grace unto the lowly.

Proverbs 1:22 How long, ye simple ones, will ye love simplicity? And the scorners delight in their scorning, and fools hate knowledge?

Proverbs 9:7-8 He that reproveth a scorner getteth to himself shame; and he that rebuketh a wicked man getteth himself a blot. Reprove not a scorner, lest he hate thee: rebuke a wise man, and he will love thee.

Proverbs 15:12 A scorner loveth not one who reproveth him: neither will he go unto the wise.

Proverbs 14:6 A scorner seeketh wisdom, and findeth it not: but knowledge is easy unto him that undestandeth.

Proverbs 24:9 The thought of foolishness is sin, and the scorner is an abomination to men.

Proverbs 21:11 When the scorner is punished, the simple is made wise: and when the wise is instructed, he receiveth knowledge.

    The scoffer, mocker and scorner have some overlapping descriptions but know this; the scorner is the only one of these that is *unrepentant, unteachable, and uncorrectable*. That puts the scorner in the unenviable position of not being granted repentance from the Lord. It also puts him in the category of someone who is lost and not correctable or teachable. He has actually moved beyond his last hope. That is a dangerous person.

    Only the Lord can deal with the scorner.

    The scornful person is at significant risk because the Bible shows us that they are uncorrectable (Proverbs 15:12) and an abomination. (Proverbs 24:9) it also says, "reprove not a scorner, lest he hate thee."

    Surely, he scorneth the scorner; but he giveth grace unto the lowly. (Proverbs 3:34) This shows that there is a reckoning for the scorner, he will be delt the same as he has delivered. One of the most dangerous subjects in this study is the scorner. *Dangerous to you, as well as to himself!* If you find yourself in the presence of this person, please excuse yourself and do not spend any time with them. There is such a thing as a "transference of spirits," and you may indeed find yourself behaving just like them. At first, it would be barely noticeable, but it will build and build until you start to become just like him. That is the way the enemy operates, progressively, and incrementally, in an almost indiscernible and a very subtle manner. You probably would not even see it coming, until it is too late. In those late stages of scorn, you will become uncorrectable and possibly even lost! The Bible says that judgments are prepared for scorners. Eliminate any scorners from your life but pray for them to be corrected and to repent from this behavior.

The Babbler

The definition of a babbler is: An idle talker; an irrational prattler; a teller of secrets, a chatterer. One who issues useless words, words that are not going anywhere and serve no purpose. innate babblings of one who just goes on and on about nothing. A Rambler of words. Chatterer means a jabberer. A jabberer means fast, excited talk that makes little sense. An irrational prattler means illogical, unreasonable, baseless, ridiculous, nonsensical foolish talk. A blather is one who talks long-windedly without making much sense.

2nd Timothy 2:16 But shun profane and vain babblings; for they will increase unto more ungodliness.

1st Timothy 6:20 O Timothy, keep that which is committed to thy trust, avoiding profane and vain babblings and oppositions of science falsely so called.

THE EVIL USE OF TONGUE AND LIPS

We have probably all met the Babbler. They can be very annoying and grating. They just cannot seem to be quiet. They just go on and on about nothing. They can be totally unreasonable and illogical; it is very hard to follow them because they just ramble on foolishly.

I used to know a babbler when I was a young man. He would talk about everything that he was doing, even if no one was listening, it didn't matter, he just kept talking anyway. It seemed like he had to be able to "touch base" with himself in order to stay "centered up," and the only way he could do that was to continually babble. I noticed that his babblings were somewhat ridiculous and pointless.

2nd Timothy 2:16 issues a stern warning to shun profane and vain babblings for they will increase unto more ungodliness. These babblings are a path to ungodliness, the ungodliness will progressively get worse. It is a subtle trap that overtakes the babbler little by little until he is awash in sin.

Stay away from people that fit this profile because you could be in harm's way from the presence of evil spirits that influence the babbler. Over time, you may become just like him. You might at first be entertained by this person but in the end, you will greatly regret it.

I have met preachers that just loved to talk, they could go on for hours *and say very little*. The babbler's dream is to become a preacher. There he can have an audience and the people would respect him and listen to his every word. If you are not enlightened to this teaching, you could very well end up sitting under one. Use your God-given discernment to weigh it out.

I have also met some radio personalities that were nothing more than babblers. When I was young, I would just take people at face value but now I can spot a babbling radio personality immediately. We know radio people have to be talkers or they would never last, but crossing the line into babbling and rambling and jabbering is taking it to another level and that my friend is a dangerous place to be.

The fear of the Lord will keep you from falling for the words of these people, you will be enlightened and have an abundance of discernment, with the fear of the Lord you will not have to go home and take it to the Lord in prayer, asking him to show you the truth about certain people. You will know, ***as you go***, the true nature of the people to which you are listening. Acquiring the fear of the Lord will keep you from these snares.

The author with his daughter.

Chapter 10.

Conclusion

This concludes chapter 10, the evil use of tongue and lips, now you should have a thorough understanding of each one of the twenty studies depicted here. You will be able to spot this behavior in people and take precautions.

I have made it the last chapter because many of the people who have actually mastered their tongue, (or thought they did.) are not aware that they may be guilty of one or more of the subjects in this word study. Not to say 100% guilty but they do have some exposure since they have not considered the subjects in this word study to be a misuse of tongue and lips, **but I assure you that they most certainly are**! They can be quite subtle and people who are righteous simply do not realize that these too are words, and the subject of this book is words.

If you engage in any of these misuses of words, as outlined above, you are opening doors that should have remained shut!

To completely master your tongue and lips you must go over these subjects and if any of them, even slightly, resemble you, you are going to have to repent, renounce, and recall those words, and immediately begin to cease from any form of miscommunication relative to the subject matter in chapter 10. Do you see yourself, in any of these? Have you opened any of those doors? If you have, you must ask the Lord to help you close them. That is the remedy, the Lord and you working together.

My desire is to make you aware of these more subtle ways in which we all are tempted to misuse our words so that you are truly clean and forgiven and are now walking in total obedience to almighty God, in stewarding your speech.

Lastly, I want to bring your attention to Hebrews 12:14. Follow peace with all men, and Holiness, without which no man shall see the Lord.

And James 3:2. For in many things, we offend all. If any man offend not in word, the same is a perfect man, and able also to bridle the whole body.

We all know that there is only one perfect and that is Jesus Christ. Just look at James 3:2. It says that if you offend not in word, you would be a perfect man and able to bridle your whole body. That would be considered "holiness."

Matthew 7:14 Because strait is the gate, and narrow is the way, which leadeth unto life, and few be that find it.

I sincerely pray that you, dear reader, will seek righteousness, holiness, and virtue, and will focus and strive for perfection in word and deed.

There is much power in prayer for those who seek righteousness, holiness, and virtue. Just look at James 5:16. The effectual fervent prayer of a righteous man availeth much. Finally my dear brothers and sisters, let your word be your bond.

Final Thoughts

Now that you have completed this book you have gained much wisdom and knowledge about words, and their power to create or destroy. You have been enlightened to the words of others and of word curses and the damage that they can cause. You know that the forgiveness of those who trespassed against you and yours, is not optional, it is a command of Jesus Himself, you are also aware that you need to forgive yourself as well.

Hold onto what you have received. Do not cede gained ground. Move forward with what you now know using words of love, honor, and respect for others, instead of using denigrating and disparaging words of negativity. Even if you vehemently disagree with them, you have no right to use ungodly, unholy words to define them. They are made in the image of God and to do so is to insult their maker. That will not go well for you.

Use the prayers that you have been given to stay forgiven and protected from the enemy. Remember speech is a divine gift of God, and that the Lord used his speech to frame the universe. Please never again use words carelessly and do not take lightly the trust he has placed in you as a ***steward of speech.***

It is no wonder that the enemy has attacked our speech. It is a divine gift from God just as the ability to create new life is a divine gift. Those two gifts have always been under attack, and I believe more so today than ever.

The Devil knows they are divine gifts even as we have not!

Many of us have just taken them for granted. My goal is to illuminate this for you, saints.

Your children are a gift from God, you have given them a body and he has given them life and a soul, they are **ETERNAL BEINGS**.

The souls of your children are going to live forever!

He trusts you to steward those children, raise them, and teach them in the Lord. You are commanded to do so. He also trusts you with speech, He trusts that you will not utter denigrating, disparaging, demeaning, and unholy, words to them.

You are their father and mother. You must discipline them, but you must be careful how you talk to your children. God is your Father; would he talk to you in your prayers negatively? I think not. He will however discipline you, just as you discipline your children, but he sees you through Jesus Christ, as whole and lacking nothing. Look at your children as whole and lacking nothing. Give thanks to God for them and steward them well, for when you go to your final judgment, he will say to you "Well done my good and faithful servant."

This is a quantum leap in wisdom for many, even for those who are in the ministry. I invite you, pastors, to preach on this subject. I have found this to be lacking in many churches. Even though it is extremely important. The enemy needs to be stopped one man and one woman at a time until all are brought to the knowledge including the children.

The Lord bless and keep you
The Lord make his face to shine upon you and be gracious unto you
The Lord lift up his countenance upon you
and give you peace

I now see you as

The Steward of Speech

Wendell Wayne Gilkey

About the Author

Wendell Wayne Gilkey is an author of Christian books having to do with the breaking of generational curses, words of wisdom, prophetic dreams, and a special prayer workbook/reference manual with prayers, many of which were given by the Holy Spirit to edify and protect the saints.

He resides in Fredericksburg, Texas. He has two wonderful children. A son residing in Las Vegas, Nevada, and a daughter residing in Bountiful, Utah. He has ten beautiful grandchildren and two great-grandchildren which he greatly cherishes.

Wendell is a minister, author, and teacher having the gift of simplifying concepts and reaching people through the written word.

Contact the Author

Great for in-home bible studies, or gifts for family and friends.

Designed for discipleship classes and church bookstores.

For questions or comments, and to order books, contact us at holybloodtransfusion@gmail.com

Visit us on our website at www.holybloodtransfusion.com

You can write to us at Wendell Gilkey Publications
412 S. Adams St. Suite 157
Fredericksburg, Texas 78624

CPSIA information can be obtained
at www.ICGtesting.com
Printed in the USA
BVHW032124230922
647846BV00012B/562